Thank you Rob. for your friendliness to us all, staff and pupils. Thanks to for your hard work for the boys; it is evident in their respect for you.

May the Lord bless you & yours.

Br. Michael

All the best for it is just a cold old England to return to. Good luck, I believe Wayne Kelly's the clap if the Hope you've found your experience in the "Lucky country" on "Clever country" enriching — stay away from the fast buck. All the best Adrian B.

To a great member of the O.H. [Good?] Enjoy weather

Robert it was good having you at our school. May life be generous to you, and yours in the years ahead. Hope to catch up with you next year.

God bless
Hugh McCann

Robert,
Best wishes for the future. Good luck with your future adventures in America.

Robert,
I have enjoyed knowing you even for such a short time. Good luck, Jane.

Robert your stay was short, but sweet. Bob H.

With every best wish,
Pauline McLenaghan

Robert,
It has been a pleasure working with you. A pity we didn't have more time to share in your wealth of experience. I trust everything will go well for you in the future and wish yourself & Michelle the warmest best wishes.

I'll miss you — my apple-loving friend — Keep in touch

Bobby,
You have been great!! Homeroom 17 have lost someone special.
Mick Power

Joan Dent

Greg Hayes

All the best Rob
Nicole

With Best Wishes
Dan Sloan

IT'S BEEN A PLEASURE
JAN x

Love
Robbie Bellingham

Rob,
Nice to have worked with you. Keep jogging mate.
Tony

Rob — the car pool will never be the same!
Best of luck
Rowena x

"For my ever encouraging Father and for my Mother who shared and instilled her love of Australian history; and for Andrew"

The Old Charm of Penrith

by
Christine Stickley

Copyright 1984
First edition 1979
Second printing 1979
Second edition 1984

National Library of Australia Card Number
and ISBN number 0 9596250 0 3.
Second edition ISBN number 09596250 1 1.

This book, including photographs may not be
reproduced wholly or in part without prior
permission from the Author.

Photographed and Published by Christine Stickley
Printed by Serif Printing
12 Christie Street,
St. Marys. 2760

Contents

CHAPTER I	**CASTLEREAGH**	1
	McCarthy's Farm	1
	Nepean Park	2
	Craithes (Cassola)	2
	Mt Pleasant	4
	Castlereagh Methodist Church	5
	Castlereagh Schools	5
	Christ Church	7
	Combewood	10
	Lambridge	12
	Flour Mills	12
CHAPTER II	**PENRITH**	14
	Old Courthouse	14
	St. Stephens Church	18
	Methodist Church	19
	Regentville	22
CHAPTER III	**MULGOA VALLEY**	30
	The Cottage	30
	Fernhill	30
	Winbourne	34
	Glenmore	36
	St Thomas Church	36
	Fairlight	37
	Glenleigh	40
CHAPTER IV	**EMU PLAINS**	44
	Dungarth	44
	St. Pauls Church	45
	The Inns	48
	Emu Hall	49
	Huntington Hall	52
	Edinglassie	53
	Methodist Church	53
CHAPTER V	**LUDDENHAM TO MAMRE**	55
	St. Marks Church	55
	St. James Church	58
	Fleurs	58
	Mamre	63
	Leeholme	67
CHAPTER VI	**ST. MARYS**	70
	Werrington Park	70
	St. Mary's Church	71
	Werrington House	74
	Mimosa	74
	Bronte	76
CHAPTER VII	**AGNES BANKS**	77
	Osborne	77
LIST OF REFERENCES		81
INDEX		85

Acknowledgements.

So very many people have given their time and help in preparing this work, both in verbal information and encouragement; bringing out old family papers and stories, opening their doors to their old homes and allowing these photographs to be taken. I am extremely grateful for such treasured opportunities to meet these people who have enriched my life and those of the readers of this book. All are very conscious of the valuable heritage entrusted to their care; and Penrith district is indeed fortunate to have so many fine old buildings as a result of their labours of love, often under much hardship. My thanks are extended to them all.

Officers of the Mitchell Library, the National Trust, the Penrith Library, and the Royal Australian Historical Society have always been helpful during the research.

Mrs. Eileen Eardly kindly consented to allow publication of some of her late husband's excellent sketches that form a lasting record of the Nepean District. The Australian Pioneer's Club was generous in enabling the printing of some of their photographs of Australia's famous pioneering men. The Mitchell Library has been very helpful in photographing some of these old prints and my thanks especially for permission to present these in the book.

The writing of this account would not have been possible without the backing of Penrith City Council, and the encouragement in the publication of this book. I am indebted to the Council for the initial inspiration to begin to delve into Penrith's history and for the ability to realise my efforts.

I am grateful for the patient efforts Vera Raymond put into the typing of the manuscript, and my sincere thanks for tackling the task.

This book has been published by the voluntary efforts of many people who saw the need for such a work in the community to foster an awareness of the history within the district. My heartfelt thanks are extended to Messrs Barry Boné and Carl Brookman of Serif Printing who gave so much of their time and labour in the design and printing. Without their enthusiasm and that of their staff this book would not have reached you. My special thanks to Rotary for their support and to Mr. Paul Henningham for his advice, editorial assistance, and in arranging the typesetting.

The continued help and support of my family and close friends have been very much appreciated.

Christine Stickley

Foreword

It is only in recent times that the Australian public generally has become fully conscious of its heritage in a mature way and of the beauty and importance of our old buildings.

Our links with the past exist in human memory, the spoken and written word and pictorial records. Such records, unfortunately, are too few.

Much fascinating and significant material, I fear, has been lost over the years because our sense of the importance of our history has not been adequately developed.

That is why I am delighted to be associated with the production of *"The Old Charm of Penrith"*

Every old building has a tale to tell and in this work much of the story of the Penrith area is traced through the history of our old buildings and of those who built and lived in them.

This is a novel approach to history and I believe it is a fine example for other historians to consider.

There are too few books like this and I hope that the acceptance which it receives will be an incentive to others with an appreciation of the importance of our history to undertake similar works.

Christine Stickley is to be congratulated on her keen interest, her research and her dedicated approach to reminding us of "our heritage" with particular reference to Penrith.

R. J. Mulock
Minister for Housing and Justice
M.P. for Penrith — October, 1978.

Introduction.

In writing this short history of the Penrith City area, I have not tried to give a complete account in sequence of the events and all the people who played important roles in the making of our region. It is more a background to some of the old buildings that fortunately still stand, to allow our imaginations to wander back through the years. There is so much more that time has not allowed me to touch. I hope to generate an interest in our colourful past, to help residents, new and old, find a sense of belonging and attachment to the beautiful country that surrounds them, so that they may look upon these green farmlands and stately homesteads with new appreciation. One hopes that some readers will be encouraged to search further into families, events and sites mentioned, or break new ground after discovering some interesting building that must have its own story to tell.

The lives of some of Australia's noted pioneers are woven into the fabric of the Nepean district. Families such as Cox, Blaxland, Woodriff, King, Single, Lethbridge, Jamison, Norton and Marsden are but a few whose names would be recognised by many. The mansions or modest cottages they built here enrich our landscapes, helping us to communicate with a past life-style. Penrith has a wealth of history in being so close to the foundations of European settlement in Australia. This presentation begins to dig towards that wealth.

One of the few rural scenes left in Emu Plains is "Orange Grove" in Park Street, home of Mrs. Sue Wines. Originally built for William Ellison over 100 years ago, the farm supported a large orange orchard.

The stone centre portion of "Westbank" in Nepean Street, Emu Plains, was built around 1865 and was eventually to become the home in 1870 of Richard Sheppard and his family. The brick side wings, housing a drawing room and dining room, were added in 1894. Richard Sheppard imported citrus species for his 100 acres of orchard which was irrigated with water from the Nepean River.

Preface to the Second Edition.

Over the past six years there has been a great surge of interest in the history of the Nepean District, and in local history generally, together with a deeper appreciation by government authorities of the value lying here in the cradle of European civilization in Australia. New societies have been formed to cater for those interested in different aspects of this history. Their enthusiastic members have contributed much new information to the accessible store of knowledge, necessitating some changes in this second edition. Only by publishing a local history does one reach a great many more people who have more facts to contribute, or inspire others to research further along lines of their particular interest. I think that the first edition of "The Old Charm of Penrith" has achieved those goals I set in the Introduction, and I trust will continue to do so. Even more so now, this second edition becomes a handy record of changes that have taken place, visible through the photographs, and a memorial to features that have disappeared. My main concern in this book is to draw attention to the beauty that lies in the area which can be easily forgotten or overlooked in a rapidly developing city. For me it is a visual experience and, a feeling to be experienced, as you explore an historical site.

In 1978 the St. Mary's Historical Society was formed and has brought to light a great deal of information on that district. A series of monographs has been published, among them, "South Creek – St. Marys. From Village to City" by Eugenie Stapleton. The dedicated members of the Nepean District Historical Archaeology Group have unearthed and recorded details about many ruins and threatened sites in the area, including McCarthy's Farm and the old Police Station at Emu Plains. Another young, enthusiastic group digging new ground is the Nepean Family History Society, whose research into family trees is not limited purely to the Nepean District. The Nepean District Historical Society continues to print a number of monographs, some of which are referred to in the following text. The Nepean College of Advanced Education, under the direction of Dr. Peter West, is also researching and publishing a series of monographs on the history of the Western Sydney Region. The first to be released is "A History of Penrith" by Bronwyn Power, 1983.

As stated in the Introduction, there are many buildings that were not included in the book, left to you to discover for yourself. Presented here are some of the more substantial homes, ones necessarily constructed for the wealthy landowners in the past. Also, at the time of writing and compiling the original manuscript, it seemed important to highlight places connected with well known figures of the early days in an attempt to stress the value of the historical sites of the Nepean Valley. The many barns and timber houses that I love so much, adding their own character to the green fields of Mulgoa or Castlereagh, or to the streetscapes of Penrith and St. Marys, were not included. However, that does not negate their great importance, especially in showing us how the majority lived, and giving us a truer picture of the past social conditions. Local and State Governments are now recognizing these buildings along with the National Trust.

Within the last month (January, 1984) the State Government has announced that, under the Community Employment Programme, work will start on the reconstruction of the old Post Office and old Police Station at Emu Plains. The old Police Station pictured on page 51 was also a residence for a policeman and his large family. Previously condemned, the shingle roofed slab timber, lath and plaster construction at first failed to gain the imagination of some of the City decision-makers. Now, this lone remnant of early construction in Emu Plains will survive.

For further reading on these smaller buildings see:
- "Emu Plains Old & New Police Stations" by The Nepean District Historical Archaeology Group compiled by G. Gyford. 1981.
- "Emu Plains and Thereabouts" Drawings by Gifford Eardley, Text by Joan Steege, Research- Brenda Niccol. Nepean District Historical Society, 1980.
- "The Changing Hawkesbury" Drawings by Daphne Kingston. Eureka Research, 1979.

It is said that individual women are not often mentioned in documents found in government department archives or repositories of historical material. The lives of women seem obscure, unless one has access to the personal writings of women, eg. diaries and letters. However, many would not have been literate, or would not have had the luxury of time, paper, pens or ink to write. Nowadays, taped or oral histories provide an excellent medium by which to highlight what would once have been considered seemingly mundane lives in the fabric of society. It is indeed a pleasure to see such works as:
- "Lives obscurely great" Edited by Patricia Thompson & Susan Yorke. Society of Women Writers (Australia) 1980.
- "The Real Matilda" Miriam Dixson, Pelican Books 1976.
- "Australia's Founding Mothers" Helen Heney, Nelson, 1978.
- Spotlight on History. A series of monographs about Wives of Famous Men, by Eugine Stapleton. St. Marys Historical Society.

There is a wealth of Aboriginal sites around Nepean River and in the Blue Mountains that are the subject of research by people such as Jim Kohen and Dr. E. Stockton. The National Parks and Wildlife Service plays an important role in recording and protecting such sites.

In reading the following pages concentrating on landowners or business people, I hope that you will keep in mind those Aborigines who gave up their home unwillingly and those colonists whose lives were, "obscurely great".

Christine Stickley,
17th February, 1984.

*"Hadley Park", on the banks of the Nepean River, is one of the oldest homes in the Castlereagh district. Charles Hadley (son of Charles and Sarah Hadley) built the home of locally made bricks for his wife Matilda (daughter of miller George Howell), and here they raised their six children.
The home remained with the Hadley family descendants until recent years.*

"The Towers" once stood on the site of Penrith High School. Originally a smaller building known as "Hornseywood", home of John Richard Tindale, it was constructed in 1824. Dr. Alexander Barber bought the property circa 1882 and began changing the house to resemble an Irish castle. "The Towers" was demolished in the late 1940's to make way for the "modern High School".

(Photo courtesy of Penrith City Library).

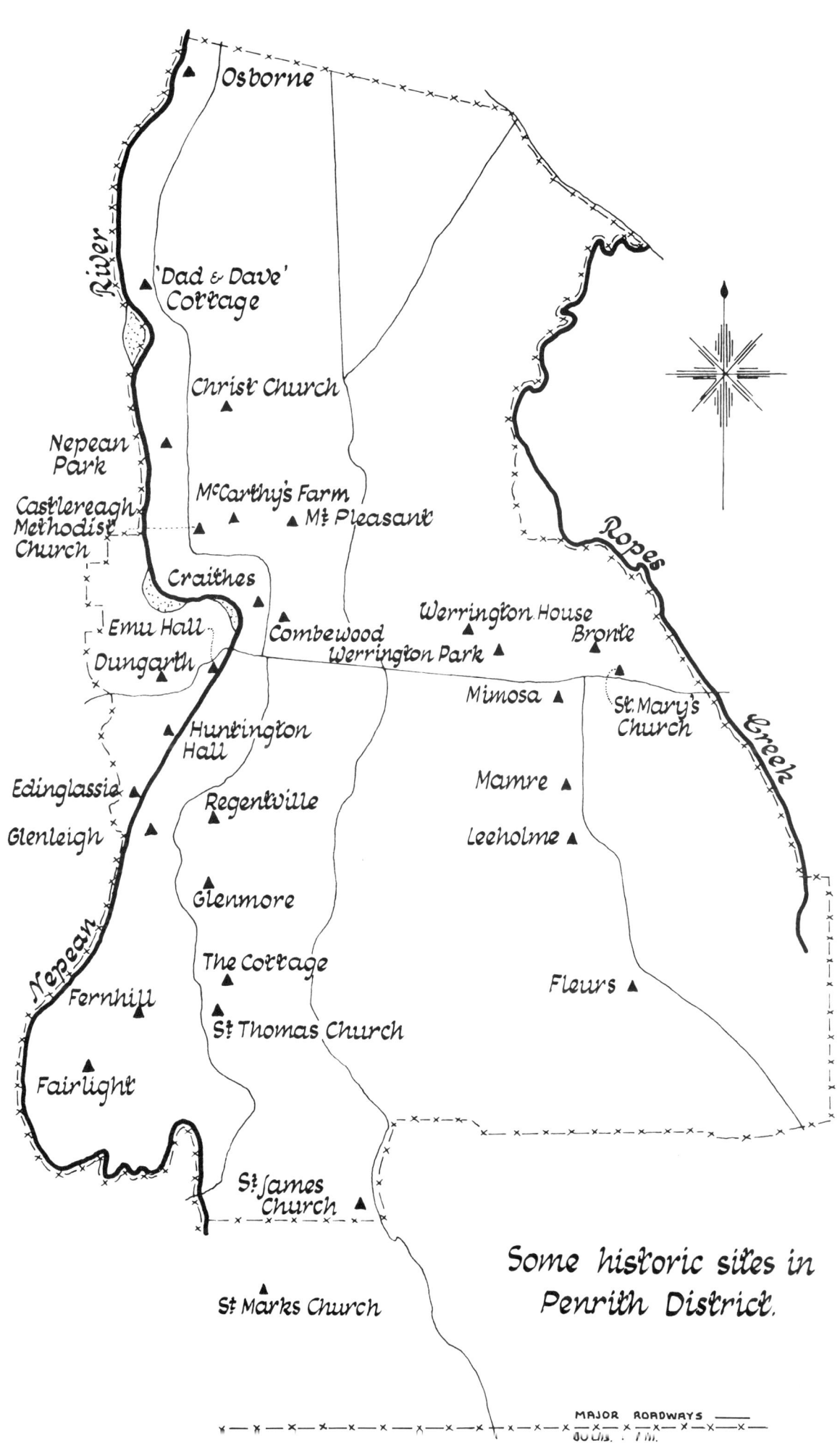

Some historic sites in Penrith District.

Map printing by Chérie Horne.

James McCarthy's Cranebrook farmhouse and outbuildings stand no longer. Gifford Eardley's sketches show where the home was behind the water tank (above) and in the background were the Brandy House and Butchers Shop (below).

CHAPTER 1

CASTLEREAGH

Captain Watkin Tench was the first European to come to the banks of a river he described "as broad as the Thames at Putney" in June 1789. On return to Port Jackson, Governor Phillip named the river "Nepean" and the district "Evan" after his friend Sir Evan Nepean, Under-Secretary of the Admirality. "Bird's Eye Corner", at the bend in the Nepean, lured many squatters to farm the rich alluvial banks during the 1790's. Among them were Collett, Collis, Field, McCarthy, Lees, Frederick, Randal and Rope. Not until 1803 did Governor King begin confirming these holdings and granting land to free settlers from the ship *Glatton*. In his "Report on the State of the Colony 1806", King described the conditions of settlement along the Nepean and Hawkesbury.

The average small farmer had 100 acres and two convict servants. Food and supplies were issued from the Government stores for a period of 12 months to enable farmers to establish themselves. There were three types of settler. Free immigrants were granted land and labour according to their capital. Secondly, there were the discharged soldiers and seamen, whose efforts often failed. It was the expirees, convicts who had served their term, who made the "best farmers" states the Governor, although the free settlers were often very successful. Methods used were crude; the ground was broken with a hoe until men like Single, Hadley and McCarthy introduced more scientific ways.

McCARTHYS FARM — North Side McCarthys Lane. House destroyed.

James McCarthy is believed to be the first farmer to come to the district, in 1794, having arrived from Ireland on the *Boddington*. His first 30 acres was extended to 100 acres by Governor King in August 1804, enabling the development of a successful farm for wheat, corn, vineyards, cattle and horses. The once extensive farmhouse with its dairy, brandy house and smokehouse was sadly destroyed to make way for gravel mining, yet the site is still distinguishable amongst the trees. There was an interesting small one windowed room, known as the "Priests Room" at the farmhouse.

In a protestant colony, Catholics were under close scrutiny, as many had been transported from Ireland as rebels. In fact, police were stationed outside a Catholic place of worship to ensure no improper behaviour took place and that there was no slander against the King or government. People had to proceed home from their gatherings in an orderly manner [1].

Father Harold was transported as a rebel, coming to the colony on the same ship as William Cox and the Reverend Henry Fulton. James McCarthy helped the Father escape the harsh treatment of infamous Toongabbie Prison to shelter him in the "Priest's Room". The few Castlereagh Catholics who knew of Father Harold came to him for the baptism of their children or secret mass service. The price on his head made it inevitable that Father Harold would be betrayed. On hearing the news of his impending capture, he fled the McCarthy home, so as not to disclose his benefactors. After his apprehension he was sent to Norfolk Island.

Early in the 1800's, McCarthy set aside an acre of his land as a cemetery — the first in the district — for use by any denomination. Sadly, an early burial was his daughter in 1806. Many generations of the McCarthy family are buried in the family enclosure, including James who died in June 1851 aged 84, his wife Elizabeth and their children. Many of the early Castlereagh grantees rest here, and family names still prominent in Penrith can be traced in the old sandstone headstones standing amongst the tall grasses of the forgotten acre.

---

1. *Sydney Gazette*, 24th April, 1803.

McCarthy's prosperous farm ran into difficulty following the crippling 1840 drought and subsequent economic depression. Not to be disheartened, James and his friend O'Brien established a boiling-down works at Cranebrook. Tallow was worth more than meat in monetary terms. The business lasted until 1852. Meanwhile, the best beef was sold to the Government settlements for 1½d lb. or to the locals who called personally ½d a lb.

"NEPEAN PARK", CASTLEREAGH ROAD, and "CRAITHES".

Another distinguished settler and explorer who added to his prosperity by contracting to supply beef to the Emu Plains government settlement was John Single. Much of his early manhood had been spent in England gaining experience in agriculture and animal husbandry. Single was a serious farmer and his grant of 240 acres by Governor Brisbane in June 1823 provided the foundations for one of the most successful free settlers of the Nepean Valley.

John Single arrived in Australia in 1810 at the age of 19. On the return voyage from his 1817 trip to England, John met Sarah Barker (sister to Thomas Barker of "Marylands". Bringelly [2]) to whom he was married in 1818. At first, John acquired land from William Tonks to build a five-roomed cottage known as "Minnaville", just south of his later home, the beautiful "Nepean Park". This sandstock brick, cement-rendered home was constructed by convicts between 1822 and 1823. Single was a hard taskmaster with his convicts; the iron rings to which they were chained at night, can still be seen in the cellars.

The skill and interest of this farmer was evident in the gardens, orange grove, vineyards and fruit orchard of many varieties around the house, while fields supported wheat, corn, cattle, horses and pigs. His friendship with Samuel Marsden helped him win a contract to supply beef to government establishments, including the Agriculture Experiment Prison Farm at Emu Plains (Government Gazette 4/12/1823), the "Female factory" at Parramatta and the Toongabbie Prison, Timber and Agricultural Farm.

Floods certainly were a problem at "Nepean Park"; the 1842 and 1855 floods caused much damage. During July 1867 the flood waters rose to the balcony of the house such that the occupants had to be rescued by boat. A famous stallion had to be led up the stairs to safety, staying on the second storey until the flood waters receded. John Single must have seen the imminent danger of his situation, for as early as 1817 he had become a subscriber to the Flood Relief Funds to assist victims of the river's rage.

Between 1819 and 1841, John and Sarah had 12 children. John had a school built (with Marsden's backing,) between the homestead and the River to provide his children with some primary education. A tutor was employed and neighbours were invited to send their children along without charge. Two magnificent Kurrajong trees, named "John and Sarah" stand today at the one-time gateway to the little school.

In 1824, John was notified of another grant of 360 acres, enabling him to select a site in the Hunter River Valley where he diversified his interests in grazing cattle. The census of 1828 details the Singles' Castlereagh property as supporting 110 acres of crops, 40 acres cleared for cultivation, while 300 head of cattle were stocked on the Hunter Valley farm. That year Single and John McDonald together illegally drove their cattle herds over the Great Dividing Range through a strategic pass, squatting at the foot of the mountain gateway to the inland. He and his friend became the first white settlers to establish runs in the Werris Creek valley. John called his run, "Summer

---

2. See booklet printed by Nepean Historical Society *"Marylands."*

Hill". When Major Mitchell marked a route suitable for wheeled vehicles across the Liverpool Ranges, John moved the headquarters of "Summer Hill" to take advantage of a favoured camping site for teamsters by the river. Here he established an inn.

By diversifying his interests sufficiently, John was able to weather the 1840 economic crisis well; in fact he established another four properties along the Gwydir River. During his exploratory expeditions in the Moree region he would dodge the aborigines, who attacked at night, by establishing a mock campsite before finally settling down for the night.

However, "Nepean Park" was his permanent residence, while his sons managed the inland estates. John became actively associated with the new Hawkesbury Race Club and his sons followed in his love of racing and good horses. Their horses were some of the outstanding performers in the Colony. Also, John was a foundation member of the Hawkesbury Agricultural Association of 1848.

Aged 66, John Single died at "Nepean Park" on the 28th January, 1858, and was buried in the family vault at St. Peters, Richmond. Sarah inherited "Nepean Park" and "Summer Hill", while son Joseph inherited one of the Gwydir River properties, "Tellaraga", which he had been managing for some time after his career as an articled clerk for a solicitor was cut short due to ill health. With the introduction of the Robinson Land Act in 1862, Joseph saw the end of large grazing concerns. He sold "Tellaraga" and returned to Castlereagh to build the comfortable brick home "Cassola".

Now known as "Craithes", it rests at the end of a pepperina tree-lined drive off Castlereagh Road. Even though it is a single-storey house, the large rooms have high ceilings creating an air of spaciousness. Slab barns near the house stand over large cellars. Construction is thought to have been around 1870. Joseph became involved in politics at this time and eventually served as Member for Nepean for some years.

River flats at Castlereagh attracted many an early farmer. Here, at "Nepean Park," John Single used scientific methods to grow wheat, corn, fruit and vines, and also to raise horses, pigs and cattle.

On the death of Sarah in 1868, "Nepean Park" was left to son Charles, who was forced to sell the property to Joseph because of financial problems. As a wedding gift, Joseph gave "Nepean Park" to his daughter Isabella; and here she stayed with her husband, Mr. F.A. Cork, until her death in 1911. Mr. Cork ran the first "ostrich" experimental farm at "Nepean Park". The birds were transported by train from Temora. Some also came from the Hawkesbury Agricultural College. The homestead then passed from the Single family.

It had the reputation for being beautifully kept during the Singles' occupation. The old trees, English holly and Kurrajong trees still growing, complement the large stone verandah and massive white stone walls. Green window shutters add to the cool setting of the home by the little creek backdropped by the deep blue Mountains. Inside can be seen the hand-hewn cedar doors, staircase and other fittings.

"MT. PLEASANT" — East side of Cranebrook Road south of the Village. House demolished.

Along the crest of a hill behind Cranebrook Village is a graceful line of olive trees planted to form a windbreak to the old home, "Mt. Pleasant", which once stood near the tall Bunya Pine. The property was based on two grants totalling 210 acres called "Islington", given to Rosetta Marsh by Colonel Paterson in 1809. Macquarie confirmed them in 1810. Rosetta was an astute businesswoman who maintained her own stock and land, during her marriage to Samuel Terry. Samuel, too, was astute in business, making extensive transactions in buying and selling land in the County of Cumberland. However, Samuel and Rosetta spent most of their time in their Pitt Street home in Sydney.

It is believed the "Mt. Pleasant" home was built about the 1820's or 1830's, a comfortable home of eight large rooms centred around a staircase. A slate roof topped the stone two-storey building. The farm supported wheat, sheep, pigs and cattle; but one of Samuel Terry's main achievements was his horse stud. Some 100 convicts worked on his many properties. Reports conflict as to the treatment of the convicts on Samuel Terry's estates. There was some evidence of harsh treatment at "Mt. Pleasant". It is said that an iron ring in the stone flags of the kitchen floor held the charwoman chained as she went about her work. The sleeping quarters for the convicts was an old stone barn, shared with the animals.

However, an ex-convict who wrote under the nom-de-plume, "Woomera" in *The Life and Experiences of an Ex-convict in Port Macquarie* paints a different picture. "My first assignment was to Mr. Samuel Terry on his station of 'Mt. Pleasant'. Here I had little or nothing to do, and this man was a good master — he would never have his men flogged."

Samuel Terry died in 1838, leaving the property to his son, Edward. Within a few months of Edward's death "Mt. Pleasant" passed to sister, Martha Foxlowe Hosking, wife of the first Mayor of Sydney, John Hosking. His gravestone is one of the many in St. Stephen's cemetry, Penrith.

The property then passed through the hands of a number of owners, until neglect led to its demolition in the mid 1950's. Yet the olive trees, over 140 years old, grown from seeds a seaman gave to Rosetta Marsh, remind us of that enigma, "Mt. Pleasant".

CASTLEREAGH METHODIST CHURCH — Castlereagh Road.

A most interesting character in Castlereagh's past was the man who gave the site for the first Methodist Church in Australia. The land was first cultivated as part of a 90 acre grant given to John Lees (a soldier in the N.S.W. Corps) by Governor King in June 1804. Lees led a rather free-wheeling life, highlighted by drink and gambling, until an unfortunate incident brought a change in his ways. Close to death after a snakebite, he swore to reform if he recovered. Recover he did, to give a "consecrated acre" to the Methodists when their first missionary, Rev. Samuel Leigh, visited in 1815. Services were first held at a slab building attached to Lees' house across the lagoon from the site of the present church, until the growing congregation needed a larger building. At his own expense and mainly by his own hand, John built the first church in the Castlereagh district in 1817, to be opened on the 7th October. Nearly 30 years later Rev. John Pemell of Windsor commented on the poor condition of the building: "The floor of the pulpit had rotted away, and I stood with my feet resting on two flooring joists." His was the last sermon to be preached there, for in 1847 at a cost of £450, the present church was erected.

CASTLEREAGH SCHOOLS

What happened to that first building is a little misty, although one sandstone slab was sent to Canberra to be used in the first Methodist Church in Canberra. George Bunyan[3] says it was burnt down in 1840, thus, requiring a replacement church. Other reports[4,5] state that the old building was then used as the Wesleyan Common School. Certainly this school was opened some time before the 1864 construction of the weatherboard building now used as a Sunday School. That cost £300. In 1863, the school had an enrolment of 40 children who were taught by Mr. M. McFetridge on a salary of £75 a year. Prior to construction of this new school room it seems likely they would have met in the first Methodist Church. Subsequent teachers at the Wesleyan school were Joseph Bell in 1864, Mr. Rutledge and then Samuel Roseby, who was in charge in 1878 when it was decided to transfer to the Council of Education. A new public school was built during 1878 at a cost of £975 and opened on the 3rd March 1879 with an enrolment of 51. The site is opposite the Wesleyan school on two acres of land given by Jack Jackson and a quarter acre from Sarah Gorman. Still standing today on Castlereagh Road, the Public School helped begin the careers of Penrith's first postmaster, Alexander Fraser, Dame Mary Gilmore and Michael Long. Michael Long was born at Lambridge in 1837 and was eight times Mayor of Penrith prior to 1905.

This was by no means the first school in the district, for it seems many of the wealthier settlers held small schools for their children. John Single had his small school near the river, James McCarthy had a small Roman Catholic school on his property[6] and Mary Collett ran a school on her 70 acres, a grant from Governor King in June 1803.

It was here the future M.P. Toby Ryan of Emu Hall, was educated. Her school closed with the coming of the Wesleyan Common School. Unfortunately, Mary's home with its quaint slab kitchen displaying a brick chimney and small oven was destroyed in 1929, 120 years old.

---

3. G. Bunyan: *"History of Castlereagh"* 25/6/1953.
4. John Emery: Teacher at Castlereagh 1913. Nepean Times.
5. H.W. King: Nepean Times 11/5/1939.
6. H.W. King: Nepean Times 11/5/1939.

Content in this rich country, cows wait for milking at the dairy beside the beautiful Christ Church at Castlereagh.

CHRIST CHURCH and FULTON'S CHURCH, CHURCH LANE.

Then there was the Rev. Henry Fulton's School, established in an old wooden building near the present Castlereagh Christ Church in 1818. Here Charles Thompson, one of the first Australian-born poets, started his schooling years. With the backing of John Single, he published a book of poems, with one a dedication to the Rev. Henry Fulton.

Fulton was a colourful and leading figure in the community. Under the watchful eye of William Cox Snr., he arrived in Australia aboard the *Minerva* along with Father Harold and military men branded as rebels for their part in the Irish Rebellion of 1798. Following his return as Chaplain to Norfolk Island for five years, Fulton was appointed Acting Chaplain at Parramatta during the absence of the Rev. Samuel Marsden. A suspension from office for his loyalty to Governor Bligh was revoked by Royal Pardon, allowing Henry to take up the formal appointment as Assistant Chaplain to the Colony in May 1810. Four years later he was given the Castlereagh charge, and the conflicting appointment as a Magistrate to the Colony.

The old cemetery on Church Street is the only mark left to suggest the site of "Fulton's Church" built in 1813. Once named "St. Andrews", the little building was brought into being with a £100 donation from William Cox. It must have been the worse for wear when Robert Copland Lethbridge visited from Werrington to give a sermon. Instead he was compelled to scold the people for worshipping in that place and promised to help them build a new church. Fire brought an abrupt end to the little school and church, necessitating the construction in 1878 of today's gleaming white church on the hill overlooking the rich Nepean River flats. John Single continually worked towards establishing a church, donating the land. Son Joseph also contributed much effort towards Christ Church.

December 11th, 1878, must have been a great day when 200 people gathered for the consecration service followed by picnic fare supplied by the ladies of the parish. The Rev. George Middleton was then the rector; the parish even included St. Paul's at Emu Plains. The picturesque little chapel was renovated in 1931, when the interior walls were painted and a new organ installed. A bell would toll from the fork of a large tree nearby, calling people from the surrounding countryside.

That now overgrown cemetery nearby must have been one of the first in the district, following Macquarie's decree of 1811 stating that bodies should be interred in proper burial grounds. One can wander along tracks through the paper-bark bushland to find small clearings with family plots. This is the last resting place of Henry Cox's infant daughter [7] (as there was no cemetery at Mulgoa then), John McHenry and family, Toby Ryan's family, the Fields, the Tindale family and Henry Fulton who died on 16th November, 1840 at the age of 79, and his wife Anne.

The Fulton children married into prominent families of that time, playing their roles in the shaping of Penrith. The oldest, Sarah, became the wife of John McHenry of Lemongrove; Lydia married postmaster Alexander Fraser; Ann was wife to George Wentworth, half brother of statesman William Charles Wentworth; while John married Elizabeth, daughter of the Reverend Robert Cartwright.

Edward Field was a private in the N.S.W. Corps who took up land at Castlereagh near the Methodist Church. He was to play a role in the crossing of the Blue Mountains. As a blacksmith, he tempered and sharpened the tools and axes used by William Cox Snr. in constructing the first road over the mountains.

---

7. This headstone has since been moved to the St. Thomas cemetery by the Nepean District Historical Society.

8

"Osborne" horse stud nestles beneath the Grose River Gorge in the Blue Mountains, scenery "so unrivalledly beautiful, rich, varied, and picturesque."

Small box pews were provided for family groups in the 1847 Methodist Church at Castlereagh.

Gracious "Combewood" stands on a small part of the original 1,000 acre grant to Captain Daniel Woodriff; a grant that was the foundation of Penrith township.

"Combewood" is sheltered from the westerly winds by 42 trees which rise in height to the Himalayan Pines near the home.

COMBEWOOD, Coreen Avenue, Castlereagh

Adjacent to the Lambridge grant in the District of Evan (Penrith) was the grant which became the foundation of Penrith township. At the express wish of Lord Hobart in England, Governor King granted 1,000 acres on the banks of the Nepean to Captain Daniel Woodriff, C.B., R.N. for outstanding service in the Royal Navy: "This grant marked by an Apple Tree on the edge of the gully and the river, and to be known as 'Rodley Farm'."

To disgress a little, the life of Daniel was one of daring, excitement, hardship and progress. His father, Captain Comfrey Woodriff, was killed in action at the age of 28, leaving young six-year-old Daniel. As was the custom then, he was taken to sea with his uncle. At the end of that three year voyage he attended school in England, then returned to the Navy. "The crazy tub" *Kitty*, under his command, first brought Woodriff to Port Jackson in 1792, carrying prisoners and supplies. The Admiralty had directed him to report on the defences of the colony. Woodriff could see the urgent need for tighter sea defences; Australia was such a suitable and vulnerable continent for foreign expansion. American sealers had already captured and kept in irons the crew of a British ship sailing in Bass Strait. M. Baudin had charted the Sydney coastline, constituting a pressing threat from France. Smuggling, too, was easy along the unguarded shores. Daniel's report would eventually lead to the formation of the Royal Australian Navy, although this did not happen until his retiring years.

Daniel gave outstanding service in evacuating the British Army from Europe before his second voyage to Australia in 1803. His new command, the *Calcutta*, built of teak in India, was the largest vessel to have been sent to Australia at that time: quite a contrast to the little *Kitty*. England had had much difficulty in obtaining timber for ship-building, as supplies from the Baltic countries had been interrupted by the wars in France. Daniel had been selected by the First Lord of the Admiralty to escort Lieutenant Governor David Collins to Port Phillip to establish a settlement. After charting the future capital's harbour, Woodriff sailed north to Port Jackson to load 800 tons of fine straight iron-bark timber, the first to be exported from the Nepean District. His land was granted in Feburary 1804, but with pressing demands for his cargo in England he had orders to return quickly. However, almost on the eve of his departure, he was able to aid Governor King to quell an uprising of convicts on the 5th March.

It was anticipated that Daniel Woodriff would replace Philip Gidley King as new Governor of N.S.W. but his subsequent capture by the French and twenty months imprisonment was to change the course of events dramatically. During the return voyage from St. Helena, Daniel's escort ship convoying a fleet of 100 vessels carrying £7 million of silks and spices from the Indies, met with the noted French Rochefort Squadron of battleships. Strangely, the merchant vessels were able to escape, while the *Calcutta* engaged the French in a battle that was to become one of the great epics of the Royal Navy. *Calcutta's* 50 guns were no match for the 556 gunned heavy armament of the opposition. Woodriff fought on until his ship was "ungovernable". His crew was his main concern during the battle, their march through the bitterly cold winter in Spain, and their imprisonment. Napoleon was so impressed by this officer of high character that an exchange with a French prisoner of equal rank was arranged.

The engagement with the Rochefort Squadron materially affected the outcome of the Battle of Trafalgar a month later. Many of the French ships were still undergoing repairs. For his action in the two-day battle, Woodriff was made a Commander of the Bath, and "a plate of his name and style affixed in Westminster Abbey".

Largely due to Daniel's efforts during his retirement, the British Navy built the first steamship, called *Comet*, an innovation that had far-reaching consequences. He continued to support the establishment of a Naval Squadron at Port Jackson, certainly earning the description "Father of the Royal Australian Navy". He died at the age of 86, in February 1842, unable to ever take up residence in the country to which he had devoted so much effort.

Neither could his three sons take up the "Rodley Farm" grant. Writes Daniel Woodriff: "It is probable that there are few officers in the Navy who have to lament the loss of family connections more than myself." One son was killed in action, one drowned at sea and the eldest, Daniel James, veteran of the Battle of Trafalgar, was crippled. His son, also Daniel, came with his family and father to live in Parramatta, the fashionable part of the Colony during the 1850's.

Meanwhile, the land had been leased to a number of people. William Martin, who had sailed with Captain Woodriff, farmed wheat and pigs on the land for four years after 1804. From 1821 John McHenry proved a good tenant, adding substantially to the farm. James Norton took control of the property in 1827, reporting on drought problems and collecting rents for the Captain.

Collecting rents, too, was a Monday morning task for Francis Henry Woodriff who called personally on his tenants in Penrith township. On hot summer days, he would appear resplendent in pith helmet, white linen suit, blue cummerbund and silver-topped cane. His father, Daniel James II, surveyor, had managed the estate from Parramatta until it was finally divided between his sons. Francis took the northern section for his home "Combewood", while Frederick Daniel had the southern portion as divided by the Great Western Highway. Frederick was the first to take up the land in 1882, calling his home "Rodley".

The name "Combewood" was a combination of Woodriff and Francis Henry's wife's maiden name Tingecombe. Plans for the home were prepared in England from a similar house in Surrey. The English atmosphere that pervades this gracious home is intense. Ivy clings to the warm brick walls between the long window shutters, English hawthorn rambles beside paths along which the occasional bantam rooster will wander to disappear through an open white picket gate. The trees shading the circular drive rise in height to the huge Himalayan cedars adjacent to the house, deflecting the winds over the roof, leaving a sheltered lee lawn on the eastern side of the house.

Completed in 1890, construction is of cinder brick with cavity walls, capped with a roof of Welsh blue slate. Surrounding three sides of the two-storey house is a large verandah supported by unusual iron pillars cast by ironmaker W.R. Wise of Sydney. Downstairs are black Italian marble fireplaces with English tile reveals, while upstairs the fireplaces are of white marble. Of the 16 rooms, the large drawing room has a personal quality in the soft, almost translucent painting by Margaretta Woodriff on the folding doors that divide the room. Cool breezes waft through the french doors that open on to the verandah, shaded by a variety of old trees, 42 in all. Himalayan cedars, Chinese elms, olives from Greece, silky oaks, white cedars, bunya pines, lemon-scented gums and pepperinas create a restful atmosphere about the house. Once the outlook was over fields of lucerne, corn and an orange orchard. On the property there was a tenant farmer tending his Jersey herd. There were beautiful brick stables and hay-loft where Woodriff kept his Clydesdale horses. Francis Henry was very involved in the happenings of St. Stephen's Church where there used to be a family pew. Like his brother, he was an ardent cricketer.

Now in "Combewood" live direct descendants of Captain Daniel Woodriff; Mr. John Woodriff and his sister Margaret whose husband, Broughton Cox, was a descendant of road builder William Cox.

LAMBRIDGE

In this region, too, was a 1,300 acre grant given by Governor King to his secretary, William Neate Chapman, in 1804. A close friend and confidant of the Kings, he travelled to Sydney on the same ship, *HMS Gorgon,* in 1791. Chapman accompanied the family to Norfolk Island where he worked with the Government Stores. A few months later, upon King's appointment as Governor, Chapman came to Sydney as his secretary. William did not marry and remained devoted to the King family, living in a cottage next to Government House. Some time after receiving the grant at Lambridge, Castlereagh, he returned to England, never to reside by the Nepean. In 1806 some of the land was subdivided for sale as small farms; and in 1829 John McHenry took up the residue of the estate.

FLOUR MILLS

Wheat grown by the surrounding farmers brought about the establishment of quite an industry of flour milling on the banks of the Nepean from the weir to Bird's Eye Corner. By 1865 there were three mills operating in this section of the river. One was near Mary Collett's school; and below the present weir was one completed in 1832 by Wilson, an ex-convict. Later known as Allen's Mill, it was demolished in 1872.

Another (the second flour mill to be built in Australia) was further downstream. Many of the large stones used to make the water race are still there. Its owner, Peter Howell, was ancestor to the great international cricketer, Bill Howell, born at Castlereagh.

Governor Macquarie had named the growing community "Castlereagh" after Lord Castlereagh, an Irish Peer, whilst on an extensive tour of the Hawkesbury in 1812. The thriving township that grew from the handful of squatters at "Bird's Eye Corner" was able to boast of two large grocery stores, two blacksmiths, two hotels; the "Do Drop Inn" and "Landers" as well as the flourishing flour mills. Castlereagh began to decline during the gold rushes; and the road westward pointed to new pastures ready for settlement.

Victorian charm in Lethbridge Street, Penrith.

Colonial Architect, James Barnet designed Penrith's old Court House, built in 1880.

CHAPTER II

PENRITH

OLD COURTHOUSE, High Street, Penrith.

A background to Penrith's old Court House, once situated in High Street, gives a more complete picture of Penrith township and its functioning relationship with the farms and prison settlement at Emu Plains.

Prior to the 1880 construction of the present Court House by Government Architect James Barnet, there existed two other buildings.

The first, of weatherboard, burned down in 1834. This one would have been constructed around 1817 when a Bench of Magistrates was appointed to the "new court house". Previously, offenders from the large penal settlement across the river were sent to Parramatta for trial. Sitting on this first bench were Sir John Jamison, Rev. Henry Fulton and a military officer. A post office was run there, too, from 1828 to 1834, by first postmaster Alexander Fraser.

To place the Court House in that old setting, one needs to picture a temporary hospital opposite, next door a blacksmith's shop run by John McHenry and, close by, Penrith's first hotel, "The Depot Inn" conducted by Sergeant Bayliss. A large grazing paddock of eight acres was also provided at the Court House to accommodate sheep and cattle travelling to and from Bathurst.

Between 1827 and 1835, convicts were ordered into different sections according to their crimes. In a 20 mile radius of South Creek were over 30 estates, employing 100-150 prisoners each. Five clearing gangs went from estate to estate under the control of an overseer, clearing farmland without charge. These were mainly the short-sentenced men.

All the large settlers were magistrates, many of whom had floggers travelling from estate to estate. Cellars in many old homesteads held convicts in chains through the cold nights; and the whipping tree at "Mt. Pleasant" was evidence that punishments were put into effect. There was also a whipping post in the yard of the Court House. A whipping at Penrith lingered in the mind of one shocked man who "witnessed the infliction of the degrading punishment of flagellation on two prisoners, to the amount of 100 lashes each". A less painful sentence was time in the stocks, and tickling the feet of prisoners as they sat helpless in these stocks by the front footpath was a delightful pastime for children.

Robbery and bushranging were common in the area then. Infamous men such as Govenor, Lynch, Garey, Walmsey, Webber, Underwood, Gabbet and Bold Jack Donohue were at large. In December 1826, one Poor or Power variously described as a dealer, a collector of stolen cattle, and a bushranger, was arrested at Regentville and convicted at Penrith on the evidence of Andrew Thompson.

Meetings of the Penrith District Dispensary and Benevolent Society held in the Court House were instrumental in bringing a hospital to Penrith to save the sick a long dray journey to Parramatta.

Correspondence about the second Court House makes interesting reading, hinting at the life in Penrith between 1835 and 1880. Heavy rains and floods were a major problem at Penrith, the shingle roof needed replacing with iron-bark shingles, the lead gutterings were exchanged for galvanised iron. Papers were soaked and floor boards rotted. The eloquent style of Robert Copland Lethbridge and John Single draws attention to the bad conditions in September 1853.

"We have the honour to call your attention to the fact that on one of your men going into the solitary cells attached to this Court House, his foot went through the floor, and indeed, a considerable part of his person — on further inspection it is apparent that the floors are entirely destroyed by rot." (8)

Tenders were finally called for 4th October, 1880, for the building of a new court house to the plans Barnet had drawn in 1878. Aspinall won the contract, and furnishing was complete by 1881. Four years later, the police station had a contingent of three staff: one mounted sergeant, one mounted constable and a foot constable. Towards the end of the century the role of the Court House was rather the routine expected of a country town, dealing with cases of drunkenness, assault, trespassing, fire inquests, stealing, attempted suicide and reported cruelty to a horse pulling a vehicle.

The Court of Petty Sessions had noted citizens as Justices of the Peace, namely, W.C. Fulton, A. Colless estate agent and auctioneer, J.D. Single, A.W. Judges, F.D. Woodriff and R.W. McCarthy.

Penrith's third Court House was one of 314 designs to come from Barnet's drawing board in his 28 years of service as Colonial Architect. Built at a time of government resurgence in construction of public buildings, before the clamp-down on funds following the costly workings on Barnet's G.P.O., the Court House was one of the few remaining structures from the economic boom years of the 1880's in Penrith town itself. The 1870's saw a revolt against the richly ornate buildings of Victoriana. This Court House sprang from an era when the public demanded utility, and is certainly characteristic of a style that emerged in the 1880's.

One hundred years after James Barnet drew his simple, balanced lines for the country Court House, demolishers were moving in with sledge hammer to dispense with the quiet charm of the old in order to build a modern Regional Police Headquarters. The old building made history again when the Premier made an unprecedented move to halt the demolition work to reconsider the situation and resultant public outcry. Unfortunately, the battle was lost; and Penrith lost yet another of her valuable old buildings, the only James Barnet design in the western area of Sydney.

It was one of the few examples of an old Court House with its attendant buildings intact. The stables of convict brick and slate roof dated from 1857 and consisted of a buggy shed, five stalls and two forage rooms. The strong three-cell lock-up, with sandstone surrounding the iron doors, was believed to have been built soon after the Court House, whilst the iron and stone fence were built around 1881.

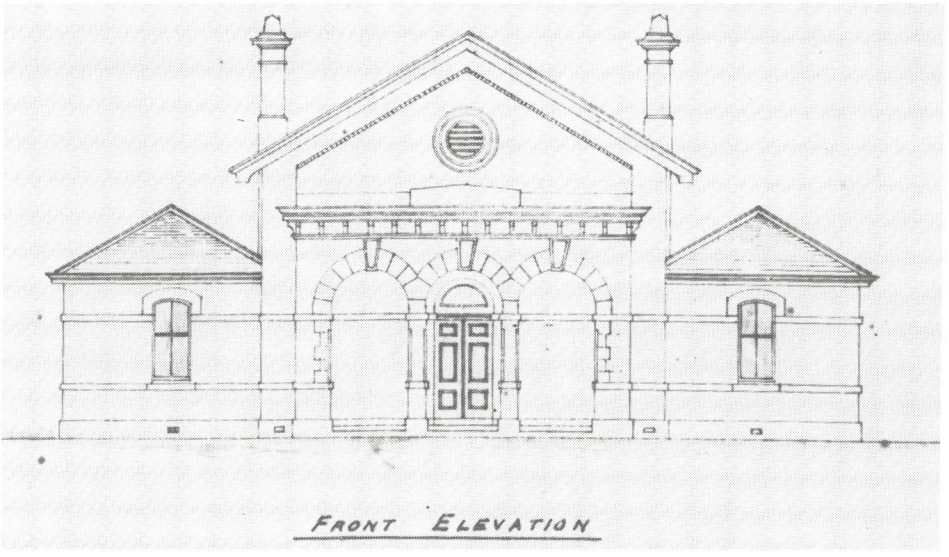

FRONT ELEVATION

8. Correspondence relating to the maintenance of the Court House 1850-1900, Colonial Architect's Department. *(Courtesy of the State Archives Authority of N.S.W.).*

Constructed after the Court House, the Lock-up was in use until 1978.

The old C.B.C. Bank of Penrith. This characteristic style was adopted by the bank during the late 1800's to create a feeling of strength and reliability.

St. Stephen's Church stands on land given by John Tindale whose holding formed part of the southern section of Penrith Town.

These stables behind the old bank have been restored for use as an architect's office.

ST. STEPHENS CHURCH, High Street, Penrith.

The church and the Court House were important centres of life in the Penrith community for here many of the settlers came to meet as important public figures.

The first Anglican Bishop to Australia, William Broughton, writes in 1837 that services in Penrith were performed in the Court House by the Rev. Henry Fulton of Castlereagh. It is thought the Gothic styled church now near that Court House was designed by James Houison. The foundation stone of the church, named after the martyr St. Stephen, was laid by Bishop Broughton on 22nd November, 1837. He was met at the Court House by a large number of magistrates and respectable residents of the city. In attendance were the Reverends Samuel Marsden, Henry Fulton, Thomas Hassall and Henry Wood. The land had been given by John Tindale, while the *Sydney Gazette* called for tenders for persons willing to contract for the stone brick, carpenters work and also plastering of the church in August 1837.

The Rev. Henry Fulton was the first incumbant at the church when, in 1838, his designation was changed from "Chaplain of Castlereagh" to "Minister of the Parish of Penrith and Castlereagh". Held in high esteem as guide, philosopher and friend, he travelled extensively throughout the Parish.

Again Bishop Broughton came to Penrith to consecrate the Church on 16th July, 1839, during which he was assisted by Thomas Hassall, the Rev. Henry Styles, Thomas Mackin and the Rev. Henry Fulton. The petition for consecration was delivered by R.C. Lethbridge, the deeds were given over by Mr. Tindale. Others at the ceremony were Charles Marsden, John Betts, George and Edward Cox. Amongst the first pew-holders were Sir John Jamison, Captain King Lethbridge, L.K. Lethbridge, H. McHenry, C. York, A. Tindale — names familiar to Penrith citizens today.

Alterations were made inside the church during 1869, when new pews were added to face the altar, not towards the centre as previously. A special Easter service was held to re-open the church, and an auction of farm produce to help pay for the new work. Again in 1906, Architect Cyril Blackett supervised renovations to (sadly) render the sandstock bricks with 300 bags of cement and replace the shingles with fibrous cement tiles. The fence walls and gates were added in 1934. The trig location of Penrith is taken from the N.W. corner of the church tower: 33° 35' 44" latitude, 150° 44' 50" longitude.

John Tindale virtually started the township of Penrith after 1824 by selling parts of his land around his home called "Hornseywood", that once occupied the site of Penrith High School. Tindale's 470 acres had been originally granted by Macquarie to Superintendant of Convicts John Best, in June 1814. Best did little with the land and sold it to Tindale in May 1824. To form the northern part of Penrith, Lemongrove, Sarah McHenry began to sell parts of her land; on her husband's death. The first sale was made in 1834. The only row of two-storey terrace houses standing in High Street were built and leased by John Tindale. A brick found here bore the mark "Tindale 1834". This date seems a little early for a style more characteristic of the latter half of the nineteenth century.

METHODIST CHURCH — Henry Street.

In 1845 Tindale gave land in Henry Street to a serious congregation of Methodists who had been forced to meet in a private home. Now their church could be built in Penrith. On completion in 1861, the church would have looked similar to the present restored building, with a central door leading to two aisles flanked by rented pews. However, the roof was of shingle which soon needed replacing. The Rev. Mr. Parsons, also architect, began renovations in 1885, to the cost of £900, adding the two front porches and doors. Electricity had replaced the oil lamps for the re-opening of the church in 1886. At the rear of the Church was a "comfortable school room". The first movies to be seen in Penrith were shown in the Methodist Church in August 1898, when one of Sydney's first travelling film exhibitors, John Wakley, brought the 90 minute show to the town.

John Tindale gave the land to the Methodists for their Church which was completed in 1861

A charming home amidst beautiful garden setting in Rawson Avenue, Penrith.

Judge's house in Warwick Street, Penrith.

Sandstone blocks from "Regentville" on the site of Sir John Jamison's mansion. What a magnificent view would have been commanded from the two storey home.

Stones from "Regentville" were used by William Dent to construct "Ormonde", once a boarding house in High Street, Penrith.

REGENTVILLE —Ruins near Regentville, Mulgoa Road.

Another important character to bring a touch of showmanship and colour to the district was Sir John Jamison, whose magnificent mansion "Regentville" on the hill overlooking the River and Mountains, was renowned throughout the colony for its hospitality. Yet there was more to Sir John than his liking for lavish entertainment. W.D. Evans in his article *Pioneers of the Textile Industry*, describes Jamison as "patriot, banker, pastoralist, politician, magistrate, educationalist, stud stock breeder, agriculturalist, woolgrower, tweed manufacturer, sportsman, philanthropist, naturalist and medico."

Part of John's land at Regentville was a 1,000 acre grant to his father, Thomas Jamison, given by Governor King in 1805. Thomas arrived with Governor Phillip as surgeon's mate on the *Sirius* in 1788, from whence he was sent to Norfolk Island to establish a hospital. On his return to Sydney, he progressed from Assistant Surgeon to Surgeon General of N.S.W. in 1803. However, he had to leave for England in 1809 to give evidence at the Court Martial of Governor Bligh, and here Thomas died in 1811. The will stated that son John could have the Regentville property at the end of a year for the rent of one peppercorn.[9]

Meanwhile, John had been serving as surgeon on the *Victory* and tended to Lord Nelson's wounds during the Battle of Trafalgar. The Swedish Government knighted Jamison for his services in ridding their fleet of the dreaded scurvy with an improvement in diet balanced with fresh fruit and vegetables. His knighthood was later confirmed by the Prince Regent in England, hence the name "Regentville".

Sir John arrived in Sydney in 1814 on the *Broxbornebury* (in charge of 139 female convicts) to take up residence at his father's small convict-built stone house on the banks of the Nepean near the end of Jamison Road. However, the 1,000 acres was not enough for his 600 head of cattle. The expected increase of 200 calves caused John to write to Macquarie in October 1814 requesting more land. The governor obliged with grants totalling 1,500 acres in 1817, 460 acres in 1819 and 660 acres in 1822.

Much interest was abound in exploring the rivers flowing into the Nepean. The Governor himself, encouraged by an account of the Warragamba River given by G.W. Evans, set out from Parramatta on the morning of November 28th, 1810, to inspect the beautiful river. After a pleasant journey of four miles, from a refreshment stop at Dr. Jamison's farm on the Nepean, Macquarie noted that the Warragamba poured an immense body of water into the circular basin, now known as Norton's Basin.

The party did not continue along the length of the Warragamba, an enticement to Sir John Jamison to complete the exploration in 1818. On November 15th, with Lt. R. Johnston, John Wentworth and Thomas Jones, a collector of natural history specimens, he set out in a small boat from Regentville.

"A rill of constant running water", two miles upstream was named "Glenbrook" by Jamison. Continuing upstream along the Warragamba for a number of miles, the party then climbed a mountain from which they could see the Cox River. An island in the River was marked with a bottle for reference on future explorations.

In returning, Jamison renamed a creek previously thought to have been the Cox, flowing to the Nepean, after Lt. Governor Erskine.

To prove the Cox River siting, Jamison later dispatched a party of three aborigines and Thomas Jones through the Valley of Clwydd to trace the river's course. It took eight days to reach Bottle Island; the Cox and the Warragamba were one.

9. Indenture from Thomas Jamison to Dr. John Jamison.

Sir John Jamison's magnificent "Regentville" overlooking the Nepean. Here, served by free and Convict retainers, Jamison played squire with bouldless hospitality. (Courtesy of The Christian Brothers, Mt. Sion.)

Sir John Jamison K.G.V. M.D.R.N. Physician of the Baltic Fleet - H M S "Gordon" Arrived in Sydney 1814 - Died 1844. Eldest son of Dr Thomas Jamison RN who arrived with the first fleet as Assist. Surgeon H M S "Sirius" January 1788. (Courtesy of the Australian Pioneer's Club.)

Macquarie stayed at the first Jamison home on the river banks in 1815. Following breakfast, the party crossed the Nepean at Emu Ford to meet the carriage and horses waiting at the Government Stockade on the Plains. For his services as guide to Bathurst, Sir John was given government permission to graze his cattle on the western side of the river, an area previously jealously guarded for Government cattle only. Macquarie was to stay again at Regentville on his way to Bathurst in 1821. Another guest was Charles Sturt on the eve of his exploratory trip inland.

Yet Jamison still found it necessary to purchase (from the Rev. Cartwright) a further 600 acres on which he was to mount the famous mansion "Regentville". The stone was quarried on the site. Suggestions have been made that architect H. Kitchen designed the house, for he writes to Commissioner Bigge in August 1821[10] of his new undertakings, stating that he was employed in erecting a new dwelling for Mr. Macarthur at Cow Pastures, and he was about to commence several buildings for other gentlemen of the Colony, among whom were Mr. Howe and Sir John Jamison. Great grandson Mr. J.H. Jamison understands that Kitchen built two houses in George Street Sydney for Sir John in 1822 prior to the architect's death that year. Furthermore, he believes the foundation stone of "Regentville" was laid on 11th September 1823 and occupied by 1824[11].

The two-storey home with columned front verandahs was indeed grand. An entrance hall led to two drawing rooms, one dining room, a breakfast room, library and study; or one could have climbed the circular stone staircase to nine bedrooms. A laundry and wash-house were attached, while the spacious cellar can still be seen today. The right wing consisted of an immense coach house with stores above, and in the left wing was a billiard room. Amongst the outbuildings were two stone kitchens, a bakehouse, servants' quarters and stone stables. There was a wine press for Jamison's renowned wines, and a large 300 foot circumference dam that must have formed part of the irrigation system installed in 1835. Blackhouse and Walker, two missionaries, called at Regentville that year to describe it thus: "The house is furnished in a style much on a par, I should suppose, with the most opulent of our English gentry and nobility. The vineyard behind the house occupies fifteen acres and contains, according to the statement of the owner, between 30 and 40,000 vines including upwards of 200 varieties. The vine is becoming an object of serious attention with many of the most prosperous colonists, in the hope of being able to manufacture wines that may prove profitable for export". Remnants of the old river stone terraced vineyards are still to be seen on the site.

Some of the land he cultivated by share farming, for the rest he relied on convict and cheap labour to tend his sheep, cattle and pigs. Henry Parkes on his arrival in the colony was unable to find work, and was at first grateful to accept Jamison's "£25 a year with a ration and a half of food" in payment for a labourer's work. Writes a disgruntled Parkes in May, 1840: "This amounted to weekly: 10½lbs. beef sometimes unfit to eat; 10½ lbs. of rice of the worst imaginable quality: 6¾ lbs. of flour half made up of ground rice; 2 lbs. sugar, good-tasted brown; ¼lb. tea, inferior; ¼lb. soap, not enough to wash our hands; 2 figs of tobacco, useless to me." His discontent extends to the inadequate lodgings. "For the first 4 months we had no other bed than a sheet of bark off a box tree, and an old door laid on two cross pieces of wood covered over with a few articles of clothing".[13] Their shelter allowed the rains and sun to gush upon them alike.

10. Bigge's Appendix Vol. 133, Bonwick Transcripts.
11. Talk given by J.H. Jamison.
12. "Old Chum — Old Sydney" *The Truth* 25/3/1920.
13. "Old Chum — Old Sydney" *The Truth* 18/1/1920.

This treatment at the coming of the economic crisis was contrary to Dr. Jamison's humanitarian attitudes in earlier years and towards the convicts at Emu Plains. In a letter to Commissioner Bigge in January 1820, Jamison states that "the present quality and rate of ration generally issued to convicts wants considerable alteration, such as the quantity of wheat and flour reduced and substituted by an equivalent of Maize, Potatoes and Vegetables and even Milk when it can be got".[14] Another letter written to Dr. J. Hall in September 1822, shows Jamison's concern at the moral abuse of inmates at Emu Plains with implications made against the government officials. He also had signed a petition to the N.S.W. Colonial Secretary requesting that work among the aborigines be continued and extended.

Jamision did much to help agriculture in the colony. By the 1820's he owned a total of 22,600 acres grazing horses in the Capertee Valley, sheep at Cullen Bullen, and beef cattle at Namoi and upper Richmond. The inaugural meeting of the agricultural and horticultural society to become the R.A.S. of N.S.W. was arranged by Sir John, who became the foundation president. Tobacco had been successfully grown at Emu Plains by 1835, so parts of the Regentville estate were sublet, mainly to Irishmen, for that purpose. "Irish Corner" was soon to welcome fellows from Scotland in 1842 when Jamison brought out weavers, carders, dyers and their families, as well as the machinery, to run his newly-built tweed mill. "The Old Barn", said to be 4 storeys tall [15] must have been an outstanding feature on the landscape to be visible from Huxley's corner (Mulgoa Road and Great Western Highway) and Emu Plains. Using wool from Regentville's sheep, the Mill operated under the management of the Raynor Brothers, until they moved to their own mills at Emu Plains. Governor Gipps wrote in an 1842 despatch to Lord Stanley: "The Manufactures of the Country are few and unimportant. Cloth from the Wool of the Colony, has long, however, been made in small quantities, and some disposition has recently been manifested to extend this branch of Industry. A Cloth Mill has been erected by Sir John Jamison near Penrith and another is in progress near Newcastle".[16] Tweed from the "Old Barn" was exhibited at the International Exhibition in 1851 in London.

He likewise played a considerable role in community affairs. In 1818 he organised a merchant banking subscription system and was responsible for the formation of the Bank of N.S.W., becoming its first director. August 1819 saw his appointment as a J.P. and Magistrate for N.S.W. Jamison and the Rev. Fulton were two of the first magistrates to sit on the Bench at Penrith's Court House. By 1827, he was actively promoting the Australian Patriotic Association whose aims were to obtain trial by jury and a representative parliamentary assembly. Sir John was also President of the London Society for the encouragement of Art and Manufacture and the first president of Sydney Grammar School, the establishment of which, in 1835, had been greatly encouraged by Jamison. Also he was on the first committee to administer the affairs of the Australian Museum, together with his involvement with the management of the Botanical Gardens. Eventually, he was appointed a member of the Legislative Council in 1837, retaining this position until 1843.

One move, however, led to his downfall. Jamison became a major shareholder in the Bank of Australia with its formation in 1826. The Bank crashed in 1843 leaving 1,356 Sydney residents insolvent and helped to bring an end to this knight's glory. By now convicts were no longer available for work on his estates and his membership of an association for obtaining permission to import coolies from India in 1842 bore little fruit.

14. Bigge's Appendix, Vol. 133. Bonswick Transcripts.
15. "Old Chum" *The Truth* 25/3/1920.
16. Transcripts of Missing Despatches from Governor Gipps of N.S.W., 1842-43, p. 27.

These large cellars of "Regentville" once held the renowned wine produced from the 15 acre vineyard growing some 40,000 vines.

Sandstone from "Regentville" highlights Penrith's "Red Cow" Hotel. Prior to the Hotels construction, an unusual small sandstone building served as a bar, standing where the beer garden is today.

Sir John Jamison died at "Regentville" aged 68 on 29th June 1844, to be buried at St. Stephens. He left his wife, Mary (Griffiths), and their six children with few assets.

"Regentville's" grand days of fancy dress balls and lavish entertainment were not to be seen again. The open country seemed to suit the mansion's use as a mental asylum but that failed. The manager of the mill lived there a while. After 1865, the Sheils family leased it for use as a hotel. *The Sydney Morning Herald* of 27th, May, 1869, tells of the inquest into the fire at Regentville that destroyed the home on 22nd May. The jury concluded "That the house was wilfully and maliciously set on fire by some person or persons unknown".

Sandstone blocks were taken from the mansion by William Dent to build "Ormonde House" in High Street. Dent then sold the property to William Patrick Manning, a member of the Legislative Assembly of N.S.W. Later the ownership went to Joseph Stanton and his wife. At one stage, it was thought to be a hospital. "Regentville's" stones also form the gutters of parts of Station Street and Belmore Street, a sad ending. The window from Jamison's private chapel once graced the Red Cow Hotel. The proprietor changed the saying on the stained glass to read: "I was glad when they said unto me, let us go into the house of T. Smith", not the "House of the Lord". Strangely, stone has been taken back to Regentville, in the form of the old gateposts that once formed the fence in front of the old Court House in Penrith town.

Sandstone from "Regentville" forms the gutters to some of Penrith's early streets. This cottage is part of a characteristic precinct in one; Lawson Street.

Cath Cox takes us back to a glimpse of life in her day at "Fernhill", on the hill behind the St Thomas Church. (Date of sketch unknown - Courtesy Mr John Darling.)

FERNHILL. MULGOA.

The first home in the Mulgoa Valley, William Cox Senior had "the Cottage" constructed around 1814 for three of his sons on a 300 acre grant to the youngest, Edward.

Family gatherings were important events at "Glenmore" when the Cox families visited from the Mulgoa Valley. Families still gather for a barbecue and a game of golf at the "Great Glen"

Heavy adzed beams support the loft inside the old sandstone stables behind "Glenmore," original home of Henry Cox.

CHAPTER III -

- MULGOA VALLEY

Travelling southwards, one enters Mulgoa Valley, home of one of the most prominent agricultural families in the colony; the Cox family. Famous builder, and road builder, William Cox Senior arrived in Sydney with his wife and four of his sons, James, Charles, George and Henry. Born at Winborne, Dorsetshire, England, in 1764, William was paymaster in the N.S.W. Corps before he left to take up farming at Pennant Hills. The venture failed, so the move was made to Clarendon near Windsor in 1804. The eldest son, William, soon came out from England to take up residence at "Hobartville" outside Richmond. Seventh son, Edward, even at the age of four, was the first to be granted land in Mulgoa by Colonel Paterson. Macquarie confirmed the 300 acre grant in January 1810.

"THE COTTAGE", St. Thomas Road.

There is some uncertainty as to when William Cox Snr. built "The Cottage" for his sons George, Henry and Edward, although it must have been soon after his return from the road construction work over the Blue Mountains in 1814. The Cox's must have been living in Mulgoa when the *Sydney Gazette* of May that year states: "Mr. Cox's people have several times been attacked by the natives of Mulgoa within the last month."

Wooden shutters were incorporated in the windows of "The Cottage" as protection from aborigines. The low building blends into its setting on rising ground by the creek. The brick nog construction shows wide iron bark boards covering an in-fill of bricks which has been plastered on the inside. Through the hand-made glass windows and French doors, one looks across the verandah to Mulgoa Creek valley along which the road once wound its way on to St. Thomas Church. In the 1850's the roof had the original shingles replaced with sheets of iron which remain in good condition today. One of the few rooms inside boasts an unusual, fine sandstone fireplace. Here, in what must have been cramped conditions, lived Edward, George and Henry Cox, with their father's faithful paymaster, James King, who managed the property. William Cox Snr. received grants at Mulgoa in 1816, 1817 and 1821 totalling 2,730 acres. George received 600 acres in 1816 now "Winbourne", and Henry's 400 acre grant the following year became "Glenmore".

Edward Cox was sent to England to study the wool industry at Rawdon, Yorkshire. Meanwhile Henry Cox brought his bride, Frances McKenzie, daughter of an early officer of the Bank of N.S.W., to the Cottage in July, 1823 to live until their home "Glenmore" was completed in 1825. George, too, brought his new wife, Eliza Bell, here after their marriage in 1824. Their first son, George Henry, was born at "The Cottage". Construction had begun on the first single-storey building at Winbourne, to which they soon moved. By 1827, Edward had returned from England and married Jane Maria Brooks. James King moved to a house close by, while Edward and Jane continued to live at "The Cottage" for some years until their youngest daughter was four. There were two daughters and three sons — Edward King, Richard William and (Dr.) James Charles. Edward King Cox carried on the tradition of "The Cottage", living there with his wife, Millicent Standish, until their move to his father's magnificent home "Fernhill" overlooking this first house in the valley.

"FERNHILL" Mulgoa Road.

Labour was in short supply in the colony. Twice Edward Cox applied for 27 workmen in the early 1830's, to eventually gain the services of only five and eight men. Finally, he decided to bring out twenty Irish stonemasons to quarry stone on the Fernhill property in order to build his house. The oldest structure was a stable built in 1839, while the residence was commenced in 1842, taking four years to complete. The Bank crash of 1842-43 prevented the addition of another storey in accord with the original plans.

A long tree-lined drive winds on a shallow gradient through rich pastures, up the hill across two stone bridges to "Fernhill" homestead. To first catch one's attention is the distinctive large bay window of the ballroom. Five french windows open on to the semi-circular stone-flagged verandah. The curved beams of the roof have been pit-sawn in that fashion from single pieces of solid timber. Supporting the roof are ten Doric columns, each cut from a single piece of stone. Inside, across the iron bark floor, this semi-circular room has a diameter of 45 feet. The ceilings of the 16 feet high rooms display papier-mache designs of acorn and oakleaf picked out in gold and coloured to suit each room. The main windows reach the full height of the ballroom, the sills are cut from the mainstone of the wall. The large dining room windows, 12 feet by 9 feet, set in unpainted cedar frames, give a view to the intimate courtyard and the surrounding countryside. Most windows are fitted with inside wooden shutters; and the children's rooms have additional iron bars to serve against aboriginal attacks. The main part of the house was capable of being closed off in case of serious offence. The 2½ feet thick sandstone walls keep the house cool in summer, while mantels of fine white hardened sandstone, or marble or beautifully carved wood, enclose the fireplaces so necessary for winter warmth. Beside the fireplaces are small bronze hooks that, at a touch, ring the bells in the butler's pantry.

A very grand entrance is made into Fernhill, up the sandstone stairs, through the double doors, beneath the exquisitely-coloured sandstone archway into a large vestibule and inner hall, also designed for coolness. One large oval ceiling window looks down on the hallway originally designed to accommodate the staircase to the upper storey, while the white sandstone slabs of the vestibule floor complement the marble fountain, and wall niches for marble statues.

Across the small courtyard at the back are two wings of servants' quarters. The work-worn floors of the great kitchen tell of the rush and confusion as meals were prepared on four wood-burning stoves for the grand occasions at "Fernhill", when dances, dinners, bullock roasts and picnic races were the order of the day. Down a cantilever spiral staircase, each tread stone a part of the wall, are three large cellars for food and vintage wine storage. Life was elegant; a new sophistication in housing was developing in the Colony.

Unlike his brothers, Edward Cox stayed at Mulgoa, serving the Legislative Council from June 1866 until his death at "Fernhill" in October 1868. Under Edward King Cox, the estate became famous for its racehorses. A range of stables and boxes was built at the rear of "The Cottage" for the stud horses. Together, George and Edward King imported Alpaca deer from South America to stock a deer park at "Winbourne" and "Fernhill", although many of the animals strayed into the mountains. The year 1874 saw the appointment of Edward King Cox to a seat in the Legislative Council which he retained to his death in 1883. The Cox family had sold "Fernhill" by 1885, yet it still sits resplendent in an old world atmosphere overlooking rich green pastures and fat cattle.

The magnificent southern side of "Fernhill" features the ballroom with french doors opening to the stone flagged verandah. Each pillar is hewn from single pieces of sandstone.

Mr. Darling and family have added to the gracious feeling of "Fernhill". The ceiling of the ballroom has papier mache designs touched with gold leaf.

The balanced Georgian entrance to "Fernhill" features beautifully grained sandstone. Windows display folding shutters both outside and inside.

The Dining Room and the finely carved sandstone fire place, at "Fernhill".

Sophisication and elegance have returned to "Fernhill" thanks to the dedicated efforts of Mr. John Darling and his family not only in restoring the interior and exterior of their home, but also in improving the grounds with sympathetic tree plantings, the building of terraces with old stone to create new gardens, and using the sandstone pillars from Sydney's old Union Building for a pergola supporting white wistaria trailing above espaliered camellias. Always with a careful eye for balance, Mr. Darling has given a new air of grandeur to the "Fernhill" site. Skilful farm management has brought the land back to viable production levels.

"WINBOURNE" — Mulgoa Road.

Only the original stables, winery and Roman bathhouse remain of "that substantial mansion "Winbourne", having the features of an English gentleman's seat, situated in country resembling an English Park". George Cox had the original single-storey home built to test the sandstone quarried on the property. The beautiful red, white and gold colourings of that stone can still be seen in the winery dating back to 1830, and the wall of the present Christian Brothers dormitory, where blocks from the original home have been used. Satisfied with its quality, dissatisfied with the inadequate accommodation for his growing family, George had the massive two storey mansion commenced in 1840. One could look through the columns on the verandah towards the Mountains and the Nepean River. State Governors were formally entertained at "Winbourne" as an annual event. Used by guests and family alike the unusual Roman Bathhouse beside the residence kept the maids busy carrying hot water.

There were a number of cottages on the estate, for the many people employed. The Cox family were well-known for their humane treatment of their assigned convicts, many of whom returned to work on the estates as pardoned men. George also brought out some German families to work in the large vineyards. Wine production, cultivation of orchards and wheat, and dairying kept the property busy until George's death in August 1868.

George Henry Cox, the eldest son, had already been a member of the Legislative Council for five years representing the Wellington electorate near Mudgee, when he took management of "Winbourne". Over the years he increased the holding greatly. In 1881, George asked the architect of St. Marys Cathedral, William Wardell, to draw up plans for the large stone stables, coach house and quarters, which were completed a year later. However, George Henry spent most of his time at his home "Burrundulla" at Mudgee, building up his reputation as one of the great sheep breeders of the Western District. His flocks of Gordon merinos were brought to Mulgoa before being taken to Mudgee. Wool from these Mulgoa sheep brought the highest international recognition.

"Winbourne" was sold on the death of the Hon. George Henry Cox in 1902. Later subdivided, it was then used as a superior guest house from 1914 until the sad destruction by fire in 1920. The stables were then renovated and continued as a guest house until the Christian Brothers took over the estate as a teaching centre in 1958.

Some of the famous Gordon merinos from George Cox's Mudgee farm are seen here grazing in front of the old Winbourne home, "a substantial mansion". (photo courtesy of the Christian Brothers, Mt Sion.)

Over the years, George Cox increased the value of the property. In 1881 he asked Architect William Wardell to draw the plans for these stables, which, much later, were converted into a guest house. Doors and a stairway fill the archway through which the horse drawn carriages would be driven.

"GLENMORE" — GOLF CLUB, Mulgoa Road.

"Glenmore", too was a busy hive of agricultural pursuit with its vineyards orchards and wheat fields. Henry Cox and his Scottish wife chose the name "Great Glen" (Glenmore) for their single-storey sandstone bungalow complete with attic rooms beneath the high hipped roof. The attractive dormer windows were accentuated by fretted barge boards. Large cellars below could readily supply guests at frequent family gatherings at "Glenmore". Unfortunately, Henry was forced to sell the property due to financial difficulties during the 1840's crisis. His efforts were then concentrated on his sheep station at "Broombee", Mudgee.

By 1851, "Glenmore" was for sale. Thomas Sutcliffe Mort bought the home in anticipation of making this his summer residence. His wife was unhappy with the floods that isolated their farm on her first visit. Hence "Glenmore" was again on the market in 1854, at a time when Mort had begun construction of the huge docks at Balmain. Mort was also founder of the celebrated Bodalla butter and cheese factories on the South Coast, and the originator of the first refrigerating and cold storage chambers from which frozen meat could be shipped to England also in cold storage.

James John Riley was the next to purchase "Glenmore". He gothicized Cox's original building, adding the southern side wing, both wings now bear the Riley coat of arms in the gables. These cement-rendered brick wings partly enclose a large courtyard, across from which lie the old white-washed stone stables. Inside heavy hand-adzed beams steady the hay loft. Great grandson of merchant Alexander Riley, contractor for Sydney's Rum Hospital, James came into his own as the first Mayor of Penrith in 1871, and as the first Captain of the Penrith Volunteer Corps. Riley's four daughters continued to care for the beautiful gardens around Glenmore after his death in 1882 at the age of 62. "Glenmore" has promise of new life in a refurbishing of the golf club house, maintaining its picturesque outlook past bunya pines towards Mulgoa Creek.

ST. THOMAS CHURCH, Mulgoa.

The Cox brothers were very much involved in the construction of St. Thomas Church in Mulgoa. George gave 40 acres for the Rectory, Edward, 10 acres for the church, and it appears George had the stone quarried from "Winbourne". The minutes of a meeting in June 1836 show that, "Mr. George Cox . . . . agreed with Robert Drysdale to quarry, cut and set the stonework of the Church" [17].

The golden sandstones of one of the area's oldest churches have a warmth of age and people past, when bathed in light at night beneath the huge silhouetted pine trees. Subscriptions — raised throughout the colony — and grants from the English Church Society and the Governor, allowed building to begin with free labour to the design of architect, James Chodley. The foundation stone was laid in August 1836 by Jane Jamison, daughter of Sir John, and consecrated by Bishop Broughton in September 1838. The large, colourful east window is a memorial to George Cox, while other windows were given by pioneering families. No longer did the Rev. Thomas Hassall, "The Galloping Parson", need to hold services at "The Cottage"; yet he resigned soon after his appointment as first rector of St. Thomas's. There travelled the families of Blaxland, Lethbridge, King, Cox, Riley, Dalhunty, Jamison and Norton, for the only other churches in close proximity were at Castlereagh or Parramatta. Headstones to the Cox family dominate the burial ground around the Mulgoa church.

17. A.J. Richards *"The Church on the Hill."*

"FAIRLIGHT" — Fairlight Road.

On the first rise towards the Mountains lived the Norton family, a branch of the distinguished English family hailing from Sussex. Following the failure of his farming venture in England, John Norton decided to emigrate with his son Nathaniel and three daughters, arriving in Australia in February 1819. Eldest son James had already taken up practice as a solicitor in Sydney after his 1818 arrival.

As a result of the recommendations from Commissioner Bigge and Surveyor General John Oxley, Macquarie had drawn up a scale of grants that would be proportionate to the capital of each applicant settler. April 1819 saw Nathaniel Norton writing to Macquarie with a statement of his property to the value of £850 available for the cultivation of a grant. The Governor agreed to allow him 800 acres, to be victualled for 12 months and to have four government men to assist. The grant came into effect exactly two years later, when brother James also received 950 acres which became known as "Northead", and their father, John received 800 acres which he called "Govers". However, the family owned much land in the Kanimbla Valley, an area that had more attraction for farming for John and James Norton. Therefore Nathaniel took over the Mulgoa grants to call them "Fairlight", "one of the most lovely places in the County of Cumberland", situated many hundred feet above the plains giving extensive views in every direction.

Nathaniel was born at Leatherhead, England in July 1785, and entered the Navy at the age of thirteen to serve on the *Busy*. He was first appointed Lieutenant of the *Brisk* in 1808 and a year later, aboard the *Illustrious*, was involved in the attack by Lord Cochrane on the enemy's shipping. Subsequently he sailed for the East Indies where he assisted in installing the British on the Islands of Java. He had served on many ships and had seen many battles before his last appointment aboard the *Tigre*, retiring with the rank of Commander.

At "Fairlight", Nathaniel led a quiet life it seems. Once described as "an old Naval man, a good hearted sailor", he wasn't greatly involved in politics like many of his neighbours, although he signed a petition protesting against Crown lands regulations, and gave an address of welcome on the return of Governor Macquarie from Van Dieman's land in 1821.

Ellen Barber became his wife in 1841, and together they lived in a cottage not unlike Cox's "Cottage". Construction was of slab plastered with clay, then white washed, all topped with a shingle roof. Nathaniel died in August 1851 and Ellen died in 1852. They are buried side-by-side at St. Thomas's.

James Norton, on the other hand, had time to create an extensive practice, acting as solicitor to Simeon Lord and Samuel Marsden. He entered the first Legislative Council, was a leading member of the Anti-Transportation League and a shareholder in the Bank of Australia.

Against the skyline, with extensive views in all directions — Fairlight Homestead

Fairlight Homestead Commands a view over the Plateau, "one of the most lovely places in the County of Cumberland".

Remnants of terraces around Fairlight tell of the once prolific vineyard. This old brick building was a centre of the wine production.

George Cox had the stone quarried from the "Winbourne" property, for the construction of St Thomas Church, begun in 1836.

Headstones in the churchyard; Some commemorate the passing of the Cox family.

"Fairlight was eventually sold to William Hellyer, whose son managed the property through seven years of hardship, combating bushfires, snakes and straying deer. By 1876, the sale had been made to William Jarrett, a businessman who saw the potential for wine production on the Fairlight plateau. The present brick homestead was built by Jarrett, not far from Nathaniel's cottage, although there was already a fine wine cellar and wooden store for wine casks built up against a cutting in the side of the hill. Jarrett added the now dilapidated brick dairy and creamery, with men's quarters and kitchen, above which was a room 70 feet by 30 feet for storage of machinery, indicating an industry of some scale. The "Fairlight" described with its prolific vineyards, wine presses, old fruit trees, stone fences, planted windbreaks and terraces must have been mainly due to the work of this man.

William Jarrett died at "Fairlight" in 1905, bushfires destroyed the vines, and the property has since been owned by many, subdivided to a fraction of the extensive lands that once had a six mile frontage to the Nepean River. John Norton gave his name to the unique Basin at the confluence of the Warragamba and Nepean Rivers.

"GLENLEIGH" — Mulgoa Road, Regentville

Some years later, the prosperous Mulgoa Valley was to have the additional charm of the Scottish Baronial two-storey residence, "Glenleigh". James Ewan (1843-1903), an Irish-born financier, shipping merchant and philanthropist had "Glenleigh" built as his country retreat in the 1890's. Although noted for the wise use of his money, extravagance was a keynote when he planned "Glenleigh" as an escape from the pace of his city life. Common olive and pine trees line the drive to the house with its complimentary coach house, stables and dairy some distance away. Hard white furnace bricks brought from England as ballast in Ewan's ships are contrasted with red brick lintels and string courses. Timber verandahs flank the east and south of the building while a timber entry porch introduces a magnificent interior.

Two Italian artists were brought out by Ewan to create the ceilings, each painted and stencilled in the manner of Lyon and Cottier to suit each room's use. There are elaborate medallions and flowers highlighted with goldleaf. The music room displays medallions of famous musicians in each corner, the dining room portrays a ceiling of fish, birds and game. Portraits of famous writers adorn the reading room. The house also features stained glass windows and door panels, fine cedar joinery, and a huge cedar staircase in the main hall. Beautiful marble fireplaces with reveals of ceramic tiles or engraved brass are found in many of the rooms, while the dining room has a fireplace of black marble imported from Belgium. The house comprises two main wings, the left, being more austere. Ewan felt it undignified to visit this servant's wing.

Premier of N.S.W. at the time of Ewan's ownership of "Glenleigh" was Sir George Reid, and it was his son who married Mr. Ewan's daughter. James Ewan led a distinguished career as an owner of the Australian Steamship Company and the Ewan Fraser Company, a trustee of the Savings Bank of N.S.W., Honorary Treasurer of Sydney Hospital, Member of the Benevolent Society and a Magistrate. In 1903 he was struck down with influenza and died at "Glenleigh" on 1st August. The solid building is in such good repair because of Ewan's use of cement instead of mortar during construction.

The George Cox grave in St Thomas churchyard.

A black Belgian fireplace in "Glenleigh."

A weekender in the 1890's for shipping merchant, James Ewan. Now a stately landmark at the foot of the Blue Mountains at Regentville.

Haydn portrayed on the ceiling of the music room.

Stained glass windows add to the charm of the entrance hall.

The magnificent cedar linen press, upstairs..

Two Italian artists were brought out to paint the delicately detailed ceilings in the main rooms of "Glenleigh."

CHAPTER IV

EMU PLAINS

On fording the Nepean River, one entered the harsh world of the Government Stockade at a site opposite Regentville. This establishment dates back to around 1814. Governor Macquarie describes "Emu Island" as "a very rich tract of country" and "of so much importance and so useful to the Government that it never ought to be alienated"[18]. In fact, Macquarie refused to confirm the grant of Emu Plains that had been made by Major Johnston to his son George. Several people did try to use the land across the River, including Sir John Jamison many times prior to his success in 1819; then he was allowed 73 acres for grazing cattle south of Jamison Creek. Previously the land was for government stock alone, yet the change began with Macquarie's decision to set up an Experimental Prison Farm covering 2,000 acres in 1819.

Superintendent Richard Fitzgerald writes that, within a year, 154 acres were under wheat, maize, flax and gardens; 80,000 bricks had been made by the 500 convicts, and 35,000 shingles had been split to help roof the five weatherboard houses built. By 1821, two acres supported the first cash crops of tobacco. The agricultural farm soon became an important source of supply of wheat from 500 acres for the colony. Joan Steege, in her excellent account of the history of Emu Plains, tells in detail the beginnings of the government settlements, and of the cruel treatment handed down to the convicts by their "ticket of leave" overseers. Women were moved there from the overcrowded Female Factory at Parramatta shortly after the arrival of Governor Brisbane.

Private enterprise was soon providing enough food for the colony, which led to a decline in Government farming. Earl Bathurst, in 1831, instructed that all government farms, excepting those at Port Macquarie and Norfolk Island be sold[18]. Most of Emu Plains was divided into lots to be sold privately. Sir Thomas Mitchell, in his capacity as Surveyor General, laid out the township of Emu during the time he was improving the access across the Mountains. Lennox Bridge (1833) was constructed in the process, and stands today as the oldest bridge on mainland Australia.

DUNGARTH. Demolished. Stockade Street, Emu Plains.

The N.S.W. Government Gazette of 30th July, 1832 announced that "His Excellency the Governor desires it to be notified that Allotments of Land, containing about Fifty Acres each situate on Emu Plains, are open for sale as well as Building Allotments in the Township of Emu, on the said Plains". One 44 acre site, on which stood "Dungarth", was sold to Michael Hogan in August 1845. Assistant Surveyor, J.J. Galloway, describes the large building in very dilapidated state with brick outhouses consisting of kitchen, store, servant's room and small cottage, plus the good fruit trees in the garden, all valued at around £120 that year. Macquarie talks of a "substantial brick-built house one-storey and a half high, for the residence and accommodation of the Superintendent of the Government Agriculture, having two spare rooms reserved therein for the occasional residence of the Governor. Lachlan Macquarie himself chose the hill in the centre of the plains with its commanding view"[18]. The tree-lined drive and carriage loop were once survivors of the government house. Now even the old Bunya pines have disappeared under the bulldozer.

Other smaller lots in the subdivision were selling for £4 to £7 per acre, a number of which were bought by George Dempsey. He owned the old stone cottage in Nixon Street, believed to be the only remaining convict-built house in Emu Plains, and once part of the penal establishment. The log and weatherboard prison quarters with their enclosed kitchen gardens would have once stood on the ground covered by St. Paul's cemetery.

18. See Joan Steege's *"Emu Plains"*

ST. PAULS CHURCH, Short Street, Emu Plains.

Originally part of the Parish of Castlereagh, then Penrith, the Parish of Emu Plains came into its own on the 8th November, 1848, centred around the new sandstone church. Called St. Paul's at the wish of Bishop Broughton, its foundation stone was laid by him in June 1847. A school church licence was then issued. The Legislative Council, in giving support for denominational schools and salaries of their teachers, granted $25 to the Church at Emu Plains in 1849. Although the first resident rector was appointed in 1856, the church was not consecrated until August 1872, when the Bishop of Sydney, Dr. Barker, travelled out for the service and "sumptuous luncheon" held in the schoolroom. Clearly, the chancel was a later additon, thought to be about 1887. Unfortunately, fire destroyed old records held in the Rectory in the summer of 1929, but the headstones remain to tell of some of the past families of Emu Plains. Buried here are James Tobias Ryan with his first wife Mary and second wife Sarah; also James Evans, Robert Beatson and Henry Hall, all inn keepers.

The old "Dungarth" residence was a prominent scene in Emu Plains until 1973. Gifford Eardley allows us to remember the substantial brick building. (Courtesy Mrs E. Eardley.)

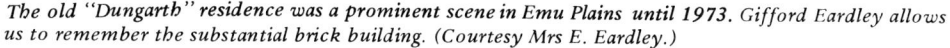

St Pauls at Emu Plains was the site of the log Prison Quarters and kitchen gardens of the experimental prison farm established by Governor Macquarie.

Cobb and Co. coaches travelled daily, except Sunday, after 1862 to Bathurst, bringing a regular trade to the Australian Arms Inn.

Floods on the Nepean prior to the construction of the bridge often meant a stay at the Union Inn for travellers from Bathurst.

Lines were being laid to Bathurst by April 1875. The quaint Emu Plains station was built in 1883.

THE INNS – Great Western Highway.

Henry Hall was the first to be granted a licence for the public house in Emu Plains, the "Emu Inn" in 1836. A year later it was taken over by James Evans, holder of the licence for Blaxland's "Pilgrim Inn". With the completion of Mitchell's Pass Road, and an assured patronage from the regular Cobb & Co., run after 1862, a number of Inns flourished on the Plains. Before the construction of Victoria Bridge they often provided a long resting for travellers blocked by floods on the Nepean. Of the seven inns existing in 1866[18], "The Victoria Bridge", "The Railway", "The Carrier's Home", "Emu Inn", "The Arms of Australia" (publican, Robert Beatson), only "The Union" and the recently reconstructed" "Australian Arms" stand to remind us to Cobb & Co. coaches carrying passengers and mail daily, exept Sundays, on the run to Bathurst and Orange. Return journeys also brought the Gold Escort. Some doubt exists about the date of construction of "The Australian Arms". The northern section, built of rough stones packed with clay has led to much speculation, for the main part of the inn has been made of brick. At first the inn was more a farmhouse, providing one room accommodation for the occasional traveller. John Mortimer took out a licence in 1841 for the Inn he was to own in 1846. Previously, it seems, the inn operated as one of the many in the colony selling sly grog[18]. The old sandstone brick house nearby on the Highway is believed to have been built in the 1830's as Mortimer's private residence.

The brick and plaster cottage in Park Street was also connected with The Australian Arms [19]. The little farmhouse was built some 120 years ago by William Ellison, related to the subsequent owner of the Inn, Thomas Ellison. His purchase in 1867 was an unwise business move, for the coming of the railway meant loss of custom. The building thus became the private residence of the Ellison family. Tom's daughter Sarah married Cobb & Co. driver James Hunter, whose family kept the Inn until 1969[18]. Untiring efforts on the part of the Nepean District Historical Society have given them a headquarters and museum of great charm and atmosphere.

The Methodist Church At Emu Plains was built in 1863

18. See Joan Steege's *"Emu Plains"* for an interesting account of the Australian Arms.
19. The name was changed from "The Australian Arms" to "Arms of Australia" and has been kept to avoid confusion with licensed hotels in Penrith.

EMU HALL, Great Western Highway, Near Victoria Bridge.

Then there was Toby Ryan. He was born at Bird's Eye Corner on the 4th January, 1818, and attended Fulton's school at Castlereagh. His parents, John and Mary, were married at Castlereagh in August 1816. One of six children, Toby was to have an even larger family of twelve to Mary Dempsey, and by his second marriage to Sarah Hadley. Ryan took up the promising career of butcher in a town once described as a "little fair with Sydney buyers meeting cattle from the west at Emu Plains" (20). The cattle trade boomed. Ryan himself grazed cattle in the west as well as owning land in Penrith and Sydney. December, 1854, was the time Toby purchased the 5¾ acres on which he built Emu Hall during the years 1851 to 1854. Today, the sandstone cement rendered home, with glowing white "lillies and daisies" cast in the iron balustrade along the front verandah, nestles beneath pines, jacarandas, and bunyas on the Nepean's banks near Victoria Bridge. The outbuildings form a well known landmark on the Plains; an old pine tumbles over the stables near a slate shed and detached kitchen, beneath which lie the cellars.

It was a fitting site for the managing director of the company that was to replace the Punt which had been operating since 1823, with the first bridge across the Nepean. Ryan supplied much of the capital for the 1854-1855 bridge that was washed away by the 1857 flood. The Nepean Bridge Company again surfaced to rebuild the structure, largely with Ryan's capital. The devastating flood of 1860 carried the bridge ¾ mile away downstream. Toby had rescued many during the floods, and realised the necessity for a good bridge, but his finances were dwindling. However, a railway bridge was under construction in the early 1860's. After much persuasion, it was agreed to allow road traffic to share the facility from 1870.

The very name Toby Ryan conjures the image of a generous hospitable person, who enjoyed entertaining at Emu Hall overlooking the River. Though not an outstanding orator, he did much good work during his 14 years as one of the first MP's in the district. His temperament certainly would have suited his vocation as landlord of the Crown Hotel at Brickfield Hill when he left Emu Hall. However, Toby died a poor man in Sydney aged 81 in 1899, having been ill for 3 years. His book *Reminiscences of Australia* published in 1894 is a valuable anecdote on life in Penrith, well worth reading.

"Emu Hall' had two owners between 1875 and 1881, when John Brown, a successful pastoralist from Warren, bought the home, and added the graceful wrought iron verandah. The old shingles still lie under the iron roof.

Construction of Victoria Bridge took place during the 1860's. Pictured here is the more recent railway bridge beside the Victoria Bridge.

20. H. Cartledge, "History of Penrith — the first 50 Years." Nepean Times 3/11/1949.

Emu Hall

Nixon St. Cottage

Sir George Dibbs found quiet rest from Parliament at what is now called "Huntington Hall"

The first Police station in Emu Plains, near the old ferry crossing..

"HUNTINGTON HALL", River Road, Emu Plains.

A home also built during the 1850's was Huntington Hall, further upstream by the River, on land purchased by George Tailby from the original owners, John Perry and Michael Hogan. George was a grazier from Rylestone wanting "Tailby's Hall" as his holiday home.

Sir George Dibbs came to live at what he called "Riverside", possibly during the 1870's. At first Dibbs settled in Sydney in 1823 as a prosperous merchant and shipowner. He travelled widely, and on his first trip from Australia to England in 1869, became greatly interested in a career as a colonial statesman. Thus, he entered Parliament on returning to Sydney, the first step in a career that was to make him three times premier of the colony, and one of its most effective speakers. Dibbs' first platform was a secular, compulsory and free education system. His powerful speeches were largely responsible for bringing the bill down, although rival Sir Henry Parkes had much of the credit. At one stage in his parliamentary career, George was sued for defamation of character. The resulting one year sentence in Darlinghurst Jail was not to deter him, for colleagues were still dined and entertained with grace within his cell.

By 1883 he was treasurer under the Stuart Government (1883-1885) and Parkes overthrew the following Dibbs government in 1885. Sir George later took office as Colonial Secretary and Minister of War until he again led the Government in 1891. George Dibbs was an uncompromising protectionist when the debate over free trade was raised. There was an empathy within for the working man whose wage problems guided their politics, and he was well aware of the problems faced by home industries. Sir George was the first Australian premier to visit England and the first Australian to be personally knighted by Queen Victoria.

While parliament was in recess, much of the statesman's quiet moments were spent at his woodwork in the rubble stone workshop beside "Riverside". There must have been time for long walks in the shaded gardens or along the River. It is thought that the long stone building was once part of the Government stockade. The long thin windows with chamfered sills would have allowed the movement of rifles in case of attacks on the encampment.

George's large family of eleven children was quite a handful to house in the two storied building. In order to entertain the Governor, the Earl of Jersey, he had "Huntington Hall' built beside the house to replace the function of the upstairs ballroom by then being used as bedrooms for his children. The Niccol family bought the residence "Huntington Hall" in the early 1930's running the large home as a guest house, from where visitors could spend an afternoon travelling slowly by launch through the scenic Nepean Gorge. People used to make the trip from Sydney especially to take advantage of this very pleasant excursion up the River. The advertisement for the Bennett and Stewart motor boats on the Nepean sounds enticing.

"This will be found one of the best outings in the State, consisting of 22 miles in a Motor Launch, with pure mountain air, and Natures' own garden to admire throughout the trip, the mountains towering hundreds of feet high on either side. This river is of bright sparkling fresh water, where you can have bathing, fishing and boating."

Indeed, such pleasures may still be partaken of today, and that balmy, restful atmosphere still envelops "Huntington Hall" as one is wafted away to days gone by on the sweet perfume from the climbing roses over the entrance porch.

"EDINGLASSIE". (Demolished). Near Lapstone Place.

Emu Plains was, for a short time, country retreat for Chief Justice Sir Francis Forbes, who had the small circular "Edinglassie" constructed at the end of River Road opposite Jamison's "Regentville". Forbes bad state of health prevented him and his wife, Sophy, spending much time at "Edinglassie", pursuing their country interests of gardening, growing fruit trees, and vines or raising horses. "Edinglassie" was one of the first grants by purchase in 1826, confirmed in 1831. Together with this 73 acres, he owned another 40 at Euroka. Through the property ran Cox's road over the mountains, later abandoned to follow an easier route two miles northward.

Sir Francis worked constantly during his twelve years in office towards the introduction of Trial by Jury based on British law, to replace the system of martial law. He was knighted on a visit to England in 1837, but ill health forced his retirement that year. He died at Newtown, aged 57 in 1841. "Edinglassie" was demolished in 1920, and until recently, one could see the foundations beside the River.

METHODIST CHURCH, Emerald Street, Emu Plains.

Very much alive, however, is the golden sandstone Methodist Church with the old Emu Plains public school nearby. William Jackson drew the plans, wrote the specifications and did the carpentry work on the church that cost £422 to build in 1863. The school and its distinctive carved white bargeboards on the gables was constructed in 1877. A creative arts centre now operates in the old school rooms.

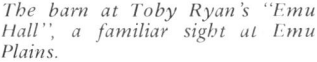

The barn at Toby Ryan's "Emu Hall", a familiar sight at Emu Plains.

Sun sets on the Nepean Gorge as a lone power boat heads toward Penrith. Such an excursion was popular in the past when a return trip from Sydney would cost 4/6d to spend the day enjoying the mountain scenery.

CHAPTER V

LUDDENHAM TO MAMRE

ST. MARKS, Greendale Road

Two interesting and unusual churches grace the highways heading southwards. The blackened rafters and sandstone of St.Marks church on the Greendale Road blend with the tall slender gums lining the pathway from the white picket gate. It was built between 1848 and 1849 to a design by Edmund Blackett on land that had been granted to Judge Advocate of N.S.W., Ellis Bent in 1811. His grant had a frontage to the Nepean River, hence the name Bent's Basin. Until destructive rust swept through the Mulgoa Valley in the 1860's, wheat was the main crop on this property. Then came the dairy cattle, a familiar part of the landscape these days.

The shell of the church is a vivid reminder of the day in January 1903 when the edge of a cyclone of terrific force blew in from the west, lifting the roof of the vestry and part of the main roof. The belfry, with its stone cross, toppled. Some of these stones must have weighed 100 Kg. Amongst the fallen and cracked gravestones, can be found the grave of George Wentworth (half brother of statesman William Charles) who held a large land grant in the district. The thousand people in attendance at his funeral in 1851, testify to the once-thriving community. Here too, is buried Colonel Shadforth of the 57th Regiment at the Battle of Waterloo. A ferry took his body across the River to be placed in a hillside vault.

A fierce storm lifted the roof and toppled stones from the belfry in 1903, leaving the shell of Edmund Blackett's Greendale church. In 1983 the reconstructed building was for sale as a private home.

Old Silos, a past era of cultivation for Kingswood.

Simple beauty in the barn behind "Fleurs."

St Marks at Greendale was once in the centre of a thriving wheat growing district.

ST. JAMES, Luddenham

The distances travelled by the people from Luddenham to the churches at Greendale or Mulgoa enticed them to establish their own church. Well-attended monthly services had already been held in a private home since January 1869, when a meeting was held in March the following year to discuss proposals. Sir Charles Nicholson had agreed to set aside land from his large grant for the church, then £90 was collected for the building. No time was wasted in starting the work, for Mrs. Edward King Cox had laid the foundation stone by 13th July 1870. St. James Day, the 25th July, 1871, gave that Saints name to the rubble stone church on the first day of worship. Bishop Barker consecrated St. James in 1873.

Luddenham originally received its name from John Blaxland's huge grant in 1813. Many German and Swiss families were brought out by land owners to grow grapes in the Luddenham region, forming a little "German community". Sir Charles Nicholson, a physician, as Speaker of the Legislative Council did much for education in the district; and the State as a whole. A member of the National Board of Education set up by Governor Fitzroy, he advocated better public education and provision of a part salary for teachers, the rest to be paid in fees by patrons. In the late 1840's few children were receiving an education, as the community itself had to make the first moves to establish a school. Fortunately Nicholson took a keen interest in Luddenham, offering two acres of land and a £50 subscription towards a school house. The Methodists finally built a weatherboard school in 1857 with some 30 children enrolled. Yet, they could not afford to pay a teacher. Financial problems continued to hamper the more substantial school completed in October, 1862, for drought restricted the availability of funds for furniture, and, of course, fees.

It was not until the Public Instruction Act of 1880, that education became a direct responsibility of the state, and properly qualified teachers were paid as public servants. Luddenham school children led a life a little different from most with regulated hours in that they needed to leave school a half hour earlier to work on their parents' farms. Mulgoa's first school was a dairy built by William Cox, used for butter and cheese making before the conversion into a school house.

"FLEURS", Mamre Road.

Sir Charles Nicholson was also a founder of the University of Sydney. Today, the university operates a radio telescope on the Fleurs property, an original grant of 550 acres to Nicholas Bayly. He came to own 2,000 acres of the rich country around Kemps Creek and Mamre Road. The old homestead now is but a shadow of its former structure, even featuring a new verandah and iron roof additions. This painted sandstone block building once formed the front of a U-shaped building around a courtyard, beneath which lay the cellars where Bayly kept his convicts at night.

"Bayly Park" as it was originally known, must have been constructed in the early 1800's, certainly before 1811 when the Mitchell Library manuscripts note that Nicholas and his wife were staying at their farm. As an Ensign in the N.S.W. Corps, he was sent to Norfolk Island, returning in November 1801. He was appointed magistrate, a somewhat dubious appointment for a man who had been twice court martialled. During 1803, he and Lt. T. Hobby took part in the publication of satirical poems called "Pipes", which were a slander against Governor King. A Court Martial ensued, with charges of "conduct unbecoming an officer"; as the false allusions made in the pamphlet withdrew the respect and obedience of the people away from Governor King. Nor was he happy with Governor Bligh's policies.

During Bligh's absence, the colony was under control of Colonel Paterson, Foveaux, Lt. Bayly and Abbott. They were described as "Rebel Juncta" by William Gore in a letter to Mrs. Bligh on the 6th October, 1809. As Provost Marshall to the Governor, and considered "bête noir" by Bligh's opponents, Gore believed they had a design to seize and imprison the Governor, although he presents no evidence for such a statement. The group did give leases and grants to themselves, "characteristic of their robbery and utter disregard of the property of the Crown". To Nicholas Bayly was granted a lease of the Naval Architecture Barracks and premises,[21] which, to an ordinary purchaser, would have cost $3-$4,000. These four officers, however, denied blame for the rebellion and pointed towards Macarthur and Major Johnston. The grants around Bayly Park must have arisen from this administration, for Macquarie, in January 1810, confirmed one 1070 acre grant made previously by Lt. Governor Paterson.

By 1814, a substantial farm must have been under way, for preacher William Crook, on his mission through Castlereagh and Liverpool, stayed with Nicholas Bayly at "a noble mansion with gardens and cultivated grounds"[22]. Then, 19 male convicts had been assigned to Bayley by Macquarie for a five year period. Cattle was the prime concern of the expanding farm.

Macquarie was not entirely satisfied with Nicholas. The Governor referred to Bayly, Samuel Marsden and John Blaxland in saying: "three gentlemen settlers who are notorious throughout the Colony for being very severe, arbitrary masters and embroiled constantly in quarrels with their servants whom they are constantly dismissing on the most frivolous pretences"[22]. These men objected to the Sunday mustering of convicts, which was shown to benefit the morals and morale of the convicts. As Macquarie suggests, Nicholas must have been of similar mind and on good terms with Rev. Marsden who came especially to Bayly Park one February evening in 1821 to hold a private evening service for the family.

Macquarie eventually relieved Nicholas Bayly of any public position, whereupon Nicholas tended his farm at "Bayly Park" until lack of finances forced him to seek employment to keep his wife and eight children. He managed to gain the position as cashier and secretary to the Bank of N.S.W. in September 1820. After Bayly's death in 1823, the house and farm were on the market. William Charles Wentworth reckoned the land would fetch upward of £3,000.

Nicholas Paget Bayly (1814-1879), was born at "Bayly Park" and sent to England for his education. Returning to Australia in 1833, he took charge of Lawson's sheep stations at Mudgee, Coolah and Liverpool Plains for experience in sheep station management. He soon became renowed for his constant improvement of fleeces. He formed his own flocks from Saxon ewes and stud sheep purchased from Lawson. A challenge was laid by Nicholas Paget Bayly for N.S.W. and Victoria to compete for the quality of wool they produced. He won the first prize. "Havilah" was Bayley's estate in Mudgee where he was magistrate to the district.

---

21. Banks Papers, Brabourne Collection Vol. 6 Bligh 1805-1811 6th October, 1809.
22. Government Despatch No. 32 1817, 1st December.

The central portion of "Glenmore" takes on a new face

A narrow stairway to the upstairs attic bedrooms at "Glenmore", featuring the pressed metal decorations on the ceiling.

The servants quarters and kitchen of Henry Cox's "Glenmore."

First Mayor of Penrith, James John Riley, a subsequent owner of "Glenmore" added a gothic touch to the building, including the family crest displayed under the gables of each wing.

Richard Jones was a subsequent owner of "Fleurs". His first efforts in the Colony had been in successful partnership with Alexander and Edward Riley as general merchants who virtually had a monopoly on imports. However, Richard's attention was turned to farming on returning to N.S.W., in 1825. With him he brought a flock of pure-bred Saxon sheep, pioneering the introduction of this strain which must rate as an important contribution to the Australian wool industry. Jones argued that his 2,000 acre grant was insufficient for his flocks, whereby a further 10,000 acres were forthcoming in the Hunter Valley. In addition he purchased 4,000 acres including the Fleurs estate on which he kept a dairy herd, pigs and poultry. William Edward Riley visited the farm in December 1830 when the shearing of 1500 Saxon Merino sheep was about to commence, with an expected clip of 2500 lbs., work for three men for three weeks. Ordinarily, the sheep were washed in South Creek prior to shearing, but drought meant a 15 mile shepherding of the flocks to the Nepean River that year.

A leading personality in his time, Richard Jones' involvement in public life was diverse, ranging from magistrate to director of the Bank of Australia. He was on the committees of steamship companies, pioneering several maritime enterprises, particularly deep sea whaling in N.S.W. From 1829 to 1843, he was an active member of the nominated Legislative Council of N.S.W. Came the 1840's depression, and Richard Jones was forced to sell all his ships and estates. However, recovery was sufficient to enable him to buy more land in south Queensland where he died in 1852.

"A picnic fare" with griddle scones at "Mamre"

"MAMRE", Mamre Road, South of Expressway

Along Mamre Road towards St. Mary's township stands the two-storey Georgian home, "Mamre", one time residence of the Reverend Samuel Marsden, a place named after Abraham's settlement "under the oaks of Mamre"[23]. Like Abraham, at "Mamre" Marsden tended his flocks, laying the foundation for Australia's wool industry. The atmosphere is heavy inside the stuccoed sandstone and brick home. Ceilings are low, a little oppressive, yet through the cedar-framed windows and shutters are open views of rolling green country dotted with sheep and cattle. The cool verandah around three sides of the house is stone flagged, where timber columns hold steady the hipped iron roofs, under which are the original shingles.

"Mamre", was a 1030 acre grant to Samuel Marsden by Governor King in 1804, whereupon the determined efforts of Marsden turned the bushland into a model farm. It is thought that the foundation stone of "Mamre" house was laid in that same year, with the intention of creating a woolstore. Upon partial completion, it was turned into a residence, although the times Marsden spent at the cottage must have been sporadic, for a man whose interests lay in the establishment of missions in New Zealand and whose parish extended from Sydney, Parramatta to the Hawkesbury.

Samuel Marsden arrived in Sydney in March 1794 as assistant chaplain to the Rev. Richard Johnson. He had left Cambridge without taking a degree and was appointed to the post of Assistant Chaplain in January 1793, then ordained deacon five months later. When Richard Johnson left the Colony in 1800, Samuel Marsden filled his position as Chaplain to the Colony, at the same time acting as magistrate to the Parramatta district.

However, it is Marsden's work as "the best practical farmer in the Colony", to quote Governor King, that interests us in connection with "Mamre". Marsden was vitally concerned about agriculture, having the foresight to realise how much Australia was to depend on her farms. In his first report on agriculture in the Colony in 1798, he drew attention to trading abuses rampant at that time. To Governor King in 1804, he writes: "much remains yet to be learned and done before it can be fully ascertained whether the wool of N.S.W. will become an object of National importance or not. I am inclined to believe it will if strict attention is paid by the sheep farmers in selecting their breeding stock[24]". Samuel went to great pains to select sheep, requesting from Joseph Banks in April 1803, two good English rams for "nothing can be of greater importance than the improvement of our breed of sheep[25]". His efforts to develop a fine wool had begun earlier than John Macarthur's earliest attempts; but Marsden placed emphasis on the weight of the carcass.

By 1807, Samuel was heading to England with the first consignment of Australian wool, some of which he had had woven into the suit that he wore to visit the King. Much impressed, George III presented him with two Spanish merino rams with which Marsden had success "beyond expectations" in improving his flocks. At this time he was grazing over a thousand sheep at "Mamre".

Likewise " 'Mamre's' gardens had no equal in the colony." Marsden was the first settler to plant fruit trees, importing seeds from Europe and Asia. He had contacted Joseph Banks in 1803, asking him to send "some seeds of choicest fruit"[26]. Those excellent peach, pear, apple, orange and apricot orchards around "Mamre" have now gone.

23. Genesis 13, verse 18, Old Testament.
24. G. Mackaness. *"Some private correspondence of the Rev. Samuel Marsden and family 1794-1824."*
25. *Banks* Papers 27/4/1803.
26. *Banks* papers 27/4/1803.

The cold atmosphere of Australia's first sheep station, "Mamre".

"Mamre's gardens had no equal in the colony". The Rev. Samuel Marsden was the first settler to plant fruit trees, importing seeds from Europe and Asia.

Natural bushland setting surrounds the Scottish baronial home "Glenleigh" beneath Glenbrook Gorge.

Dining, in a country atmosphere, to the tunes of convict tales, is fun at "The Settlers" - Mulgoa's old police station.

Whilst previous governors had looked to Marsden for advice, Macquarie conflicted often with the Reverend gentleman, even though he continued to give substantial grants to accommodate his increasing flocks. Marsden was opposed to the appointment of a military governor from the outset. He felt Macquarie would have little sympathy for the needs of a settlement based on agriculture. Nor did his opinion change. Marsden aggravated the situation through his association with William Wilberforce, who initiated many attacks on Macquarie in the British Parliament. The apparently seditious nature of these attacks led the Governor to state in the presence of official witnesses that Marsden was "unworthy of mixing in private society or intercourse with me, I never wish to see you except on public duty"[27]. Macquarie several times dismissed him of his duties as magistrate. In a Government Despatch of 1817, Macquarie marks him as being discontent. Continuing he says, "Some years ago and for the express purpose of preventing severe punishments from being inflicted in the Interior Districts by the magistrates, I directed them to send me quarterly returns of all persons confined, tried and punished by their authority. In those received from Rev. S. Marsden as Senior Magistrate of Parramatta, I have invariably found that the punishments inflicted by his authority are much more severe than those of many other magistrates in the colony". It is true too that the convicts at "Mamre" had to work hard; there is report of one poor unfortunate being shackled to a plough. Marsden had the bell from his first chapel in Parramatta installed at "Mamre" to call the convicts to meals and prayers.

However, Eric Ramsden[27] feels that "the Marsden home was the centre of some culture when opportunities for intercourse between people of similar tastes were few and far between. The moral standard that he set was one that he maintained himself in a community that had little respect for what the Marsden family stood." Still he was a wilfull character, with little tolerance for opposition to his plans or human frailty, a fact that made life difficult for his son Charles, a fun-loving person inclined towards the occasional practical joke.

Charles Simeon Marsden came to live at "Mamre" soon after his return from school in England in 1823, whilst his parents and sisters lived in Parramatta. Samuel had sent him to a Welsh religious college, then medical school, but Charles had no wish to become either doctor or minister, and was happy to return to the rural life at "Mamre". Here he lived with his wife Elizabeth Howard Brabyn, daughter of a Captain in the N.S.W. Corps. The property formally became his on Samuel Marsden's death in 1838. The glory of "Mamre" began to die too, the Marsden fortunes were disappearing for the genial Charles was something of a spendthrift. The market price for wool dropped, and the 1840's bank crisis hit the farm badly. The land was sold gradually in pieces such that none remained in the family at the death of Charles in 1868.

Possibly around 1840 the homestead was sold to Richard Rouse of Rouse Hill. His three daughters allowed to draw lots for the three family properties and the youngest, Elizabeth, drew the lot that gave her "Mamre" as a dowry on her marriage to the Honourable Robert Fitzgerald, M.L.C. of Windsor in 1841. Under this family, whose descendants have owned "Mamre" until recently, the farm again thrived as a horse stud. A tanbark race course was made, and it is here, that "Archer", winner of the first and second Melbourne Cup was trained. Annual horse sales on the property mounted to thousands of pounds and hundreds of horses changing hands between buyers from as

27. "Marsden and the South Seas" Eric Ramsden.

far away as Melbourne and Adelaide. Even today, though the 20 acres of orchards have gone, there is still a small flock of sheep grazing on the site of Australia's first sheep station.

"LEEHOLME"

A near neighbour was Gregory Blaxland at his house "Leeholme" which was situated on the left bank of South Creek. Gregory and his brother John had sold their extensive English estates in order to come to the colony amongst the first free settlers; and were willing to invest £6000 of their capital. John's grant was on the western side of the Nepean near Blaxland's Crossing, where ruins of the old brewery and flourmill still stand.

The plaque on Luddenham Road near "Leeholme" commemorates the beginning of the Blue Mountains Crossing in 1813. The narrative for Tuesday, 11th May, 1813 reads: "Mr. Gregory Blaxland, Mr. William Wentworth and Lieutenant Lawson with four servants, five Dogs and four horses loaded with provisions, ammunition and other necessaries, took their departure to endeavour to explore the interior of the country and to effect a passage over the Blue Mountains"

Gregory Blaxland - arrived in Sydney 11th April 1806

Light from an eclipsing sun shines down on "Werrington Park" standing as a reminder to Governor Bligh's outspoken daughter, Mary. Her husband, Sir Maurice O'Connell was Major-General Commanding the Forces in N.S.W.

"Mimosa" was built in St Marys by James Sainsbury for tanner Andrew Thompson in 1886.

On the hill at St Marys is the resting place of Governor King's family who were much involved with construction of the church.

Stained glass windows inside St Marys.

CHAPTER VI

ST. MARYS
"WERRINGTON PARK", Great Western Highway.

Gracing the hill at Werrington Park is the stuccoed brick home once belonging to Sir Maurice O'Connell and his wife Mary, daughter of Governor Bligh. Mary was a headstrong young woman whose open hostility towards her father's opponents were even an embarrassment to the Governor. In January 1806 King had given a 600 acre grant to her, but her husband, Lt. Putland, died within two years. Just prior to her expected departure for England with Governor Bligh, Mary decided to marry Lt. Colonel Maurice O'Connell. Maurice had arrived with his first battalion of the 73rd Regiment with Governor Macquarie. O'Connell was commissioned as Lt. Governor in January 1810, then on May 8th, married Mary at Government House. The day before, O'Connell was granted 2500 acres of land which he called Riverston. In June, as a wedding present, a further grant of 1055 acres was made to Mary adjoining her original "Frogmore" grant.

However, favour with Macquarie was short lived. August 1813, and the Governor was preparing the 73rd Regiment and O'Connell for transfer to Ceylon. Mary's continued resentment towards people and families "the least inimical of her father's government" was making life difficult. Though the Lt. Colonel was a "naturally very well disposed young man, he allows himself to be a good deal influenced by his wife's strong-rooted prejudices".

Whilst away, he was knighted in 1834. The estate was managed by Major Druitt until the O'Connells returned in 1838, with Maurice as Major General Commanding the Forces in N.S.W. On arrival, he was appointed to the Executive and Legislative Councils, and again Mary's disruption was a constant concern. Sir Maurice was nominated to the Legislative Council in 1843-1844, and administered the government between the departure of Gipps and the instatement of Fitzroy.

Due to demands of parliament, the O'Connells could not have been able to stay often at "Werrington Park'. The house was sold in 1840 to Mr. Hockey and 1,000 acres subdivided in 1842. Sir Maurice died at their Potts Point home in 1848, whereupon Mary returned to Paris, then England, outliving her husband by 16 years.

"Werrington Park" had a number of owners in the following years; Charles Hadley was in occupation from 1856 to 1881. Since 1954, the N.S.W. Government has run a school for mentally handicapped boys here. A number of additions have since changed the character of the original building, even the upper storey was built later. Old pepperina trees hang low over the deep verandah, providing a cool restful haven on the hill.

Sir Maurice O'Connell was the first to give any formality to the small settlement of South Creek clustered around the main road and river's bank. His was the first of the large estates nearby to be subdivided and put up for sale on May 20th, 1842, in 10 to 50 acre lots. O'Connell envisaged a township along English lines featuring a central market square for which 3½ acres were set aside. With a later addition from tanner Alfred Alcock in 1892, this became today's familiar five acre Victoria Park. Sir Maurice gave the names to Princess Mary Street, Albert Street (now Pages Road) and Putland Street. The posters advertising this sale used the name "St. Mary" publicly for the first time, probably making the township the only one in Australia to be called after its church. In 1856, Andrew McCullock further subdivided his 50 acre portion bought from the "St. Mary's Estate", enabling growth of the village away from the main road. Another major subdivision took place around Parkes Platform (now Werrington Station) in December 1885, where land was cleared on the Lethbridge and former O'Connell estates and sold in lots with 125 feet frontage by 592 feet deep. The advertisement states that the "soil has been under cultivation and there are splendid vineyards in the neighbourhood"[28]. A special train ran to take prospective buyers holding their £2 deposits, to inspect the site.

Governor Phillip Gidley King gave his three daughters and son, Phillip Parker, grants totalling 2,340 acres in the vicinity of St. Marys. The governor's wife, Anna, controlled them as one from their home "Dunheved" named after a 13th century castle in Cornwall. Now no longer in existence, it was once among the finest farms in the colony, extensively cultivated and well stocked. Macquarie had occasion twice to commend Mrs. King on the fine cattle herds.

Governor and Mrs. King returned to England where he died in 1808. However, it was not until 1832 that Anna could return to the country she loved. In the meantime, the estate had been managed by Rowland Hassall, and also Phillip Parker King with his wife Harriet Lethbridge. Phillip Parker had contributed significantly to exploration and charting of the coastline, giving the first report on the area around Port Darwin. While in England in 1823, he knew he would return to his grants in N.S.W. on which ran 850 cattle, 40 horses, 1800 sheep, 100 pigs. Phillip and his mother returned to the colony in 1832. Yet, his political and naval career dominated his life, such that he became the first Australian-born Admiral of Great Britain, and the first to gain eminence in the world outside N.S.W. He died in 1856 and was buried in St. Marys Church cemetery.

ST. MARYS CHURCH, Great Western Highway

Phillip Parker King gave the land on which St Marys was to be built in a style similar to the St. Mary Magdalene Church in Dunheved, to a design drawn by architect Francis Clarke. The period between 1836 and 1850 marks the greatest church building period in the history of N.S.W. In 1837, Bishop Broughton reported that 82 additional churches were in the course of erection. The foundation stone to St. Mary's was laid by the Bishop on 22nd November, 1837, the same day as St. Stephens' had begun in Penrith. Clay was quarried from the Dunheved estate, and the church was completed in 1840, when Bishop Broughton returned for the April consecration service. Unfortunately, the bricks have been cement-rendered and the slate roof replaced with tiles. Inside, the north wall bears a fine glass window to the memory of John King Lethbridge.

The cemetery has many impressive headstones marking the passing of important characters in Australian History; Phillip Parker King, Anna King, her daughter Mary, the King Lethbridge family and many other well known St. Marys family names; Hacketts, Charkers, Turners, Beacrofts.

28. King's Papers Vol. 6 Miscellaneous.

"Werrington House" was three years in construction before Robert Copland Lethbridge and his wife, Mary King, daughter of the Governor, could take up residence.

Beautiful Georgian Architecture in the doorway of "Werrington House".

Particularly adept masonary shows the fine grain in the sandstone

"Bronte" in St Marys was the home of famous wagon builder James Bennett.

A restored Bennett Wagon on its last journey to its monumental stand in St Marys.

"WERRINGTON HOUSE", Rugby Street, Werrington

Mary King, youngest daughter of the Governor, married Robert Copland Lethbridge and on their arrival in Sydney in 1827 they decided to take up residence on Mary's grant. Here they built a formal, two-storey colonial house with an open front facade. The verandahs were restricted to the rear and side sections of the home. Work commenced in 1829, to be finished by 1832. The sandstone, quarried nearby, displays unusually fine masonary, especially the smoothly cut blocks in the front of the house. To maintain the symmetry so important in Georgian architecture, a simulated window has been built into the front facade. At one time a rubble stone kitchen at the rear formed a wing of an enclosed courtyard, the other wings have since been destroyed. The small wooden cottage in the grounds is of a similar period.

"Werrington House" has remained in the Lethbridge family. Sir Henry Parkes rented the estate from 1860 to 1871. Whilst travelling in England at that time, a friend, Dadley, saw the resemblance of the cottage at Stoneleigh — where Parkes spent his early childhood — to those surroundings of "Werrington House".

"MIMOSA", Pages Road, St. Marys

With the country estates raising such fine cattle, it is little wonder that tanning became a major industry in St. Marys from the 1840's until 1950's. Thomas Paskin and Alexandra Simpson were pioneer tanners in the late 1840's, then came John Page, regarded as the "father" of the St. Mary's industry. Irishman Samuel Thompson began his yard on the east bank of South Creek. His son, Andrew, born in 1852, was to own the largest tannery in N.S.W. in 1906. Even at the age of ten, young Andrew helped at the South Creek tannery. Due to its frequent flooding he decided to re-site his own pits on higher ground. A friend helped him buy his first hides, and the continued care with which he selected the quality hides eventually won him acclaim both locally and overseas. At the 1900 London Exhibition he was awarded first prize for his light sole leather. A scientific tannery replaced the old factory destroyed by fire in 1899. Employing 25 people and treating 520 hides a week, it was renowned for its cleanliness, efficiency and careful management.

Around 1886, Thompson had the gracious home "Mimosa" built for him by James Sainsbury, who had the bricks made on his own property. The two-storey home with its white wrought-iron lace verandahs stands brilliantly overlooking Victoria Park. On Andrew's death in 1918, son Herbert continued the good name in tanning. At the peak of output during World War I, over 400 men were employed at the seven tanneries at St. Marys and Kingswood. Other names such as Desborough, Herford, Jones, Hamilton, Webb, Forsyth, Saddington, Alcock and Anschau have their connection with the industry, while tanner and bootmaker Brell operated until 1934, with Millen being the last to close down in 1956.

Autumn at "Osborne" farm down on the banks of the Nepean, at Agnes Banks.

Along Castlereagh Road stands this timber slab and iron cottage over 100 years old,

"BRONTE", Gidley Street, St. Marys

The waggon-building industry also won St. Marys wide acclaim. James William Bennett came to St. Marys around 1857 and began work as a wheelwright opposite Victoria Square. Later entering the hotel business, he continued building waggons at the rear of the "Volunteer Hotel" (the corner of Princess Street and the Great Western Highway). Here sons George and James learnt the trade, enabling them to manage the wheelwright and blacksmith's shop on their father's death in 1908.

George expanded the business, opening a shop in Queen Street where the brothers operated in partnership until 1875. Then James decided to open his own shop further south in Queen Street. Independent operation was maintained until George retired in 1920. James died a year later but two of his sons in turn kept up the good work. The 1920's saw the construction of the largest waggon, the rear wheels of which were 6½ feet tall. Bennett waggons were famous throughout Australia in their role hauling bales of wool to the coast. In 1922 a team of horses pulled 33 tons of wheat on a 15 ton model waggon some seven miles.

The waggons were exported to Africa, America, Pacific Islands and to North-west Australia. One of the old waggons has been refurbished and stands as a monument to the Bennett family in South Creek Park. The Victorian two-storey home, "Bronte" in Gidley Street, St. Marys was built in 1889 by James Sainsbury for James Bennett II, and it was here James William Bennett I lived in retirement. "Bronte" had been occupied by the Bennett family for four generations until its recent sale".

Iron lace at "Craithes"

CHAPTER VII

AGNES BANKS
OSBORNE FARM

"Agnes Banks" after his mother Agnes Hillson, was the name Andrew Thompson gave to his 78 acre grant on the banks of the Nepean in 1804. A further 200 acres, stretching down to Yarramundi Lagoon came his way three months later. This man Macquarie described as the "Father of Windsor" had been transported as a convict in 1792. Following his pardon five years later, he rose to become a "most respectable and Opulent Free Settler".[29]

Governors Bligh and Hunter, as well as the new settlers along the Hawkesbury, were impressed with this Head Constable, who many times saved lives and property during the disastrous floods. Between 1800 and 1806, he developed as trader, toll-keeper, brewer, farmer, pastoralist, manufacturer, ship-builder and manager of a salt works. In 1802, he constructed a floating bridge across South Creek with the authorisation to collect tolls. The centre of his business was a granary to which wheat was brought from surrounding farms, the profits from which were used to equip his ships for New Zealand, the Pacific Islands, Tasmania and Newcastle.

Andrew Thompson strongly supported Bligh during the Rum Rebellion, and was consequently dismissed as Chief Constable after the coup. Richard Fitzgerald then took Thompson's post at Windsor. However, Macquarie showed his respect for Andrew by appointing him Chief magistrate of the Hawkesbury, the first emancipist to hold a magistrate's position. At the age of 37, Andrew died in 1810. His was the first burial at St. Matthews, Windsor. Macquarie named Thompson Square in Windsor after him for it was here that Andrew had made his home.

Even though Andrew had not lived on his "Agnes Banks" grant, he had kept a continuing interest in the development of his farm, leasing it out to tenant farmers. One of the first, Joseph Nobbs paid £80 a year rent. The property was not to stay in the family, for although Thompson had willed half of his propoerty to his Scottish relatives, they were not interested in taking on the farming challenge in a new land. The rest of the property was divided between his good friend Simeon Lord and Governor Macquarie who had promoted him to the position of Magistrate.

The Governor's Aide-de-Camp, Captain Anthill and Thomas Moore, founder of the Moore Theological College, leased the land until it was sold at auction in 1815. The Sydney Gazette of January 28th writes after the sale, that "'Agnes Banks' — one of the most favourite objects of Mr. Thompson's early attention and application, was sold for upwards of £500 and reckoning upon the enchanting situation of the farm and the capability it affords of very considerable improvements."

The neat two-storey white stuccoed sandstone house, "Osborne", that nestles down by the River on Thompson's grant is thought to have been constructed in the 1820's. An 1812 sales advertisement made no mention of any buildings on the estate. A sale was finally made in 1815 to Governor Macquarie's Secretary, T.J. Campbell. However, the *Sydney Gazette* advertised for tenants in 1823, describing two good farm houses, the largest and best peachery in the colony and land of superior fertility set in scenery "so unrivalledly beautiful, rich, varied and picturesque".

Superlatives never end for this land as the Gazette again states that "The lovers of retirement and of picturesque objects of nature will soon find peculiar satisfaction in surveying the romantic ascents of the Blue Mountains and in tracing its surrounding scenery."

---

29. Historical Records of N.S.W., Vol. 7 p 347.
    Macquarie's Despatch to Liverpool, October 27th 1810.

Increased sophistication in the Cox family homesteads. "Hobartville" was the residence of W'm Cox

From the rear — panoramic views over the river flats to the Blue Mountains.

Upstairs bedroom - "Hobartville".

Soft glow over the entrance hall and stone stairway

The sitting room and main bedroom upstairs look towards the Nepean

"Hobartville" was built in 1828 to a design by Francis Greenway

Afterword.

How tenuous is our hold on our heritage. How carefully must we cherish the moments we enjoy at the sight of an old white farmhouse on the river flats, or wonder at the sight of past detailed craftsmanship. Whilst this book was being published, I heard of the tragic outbreak of a fire at "Osborne", a fire that destroyed the upper storey of this beautiful home. Thankfully, no one was hurt, save the sorrow of the loss of so many precious items and memories. It is hoped that help may be forthcoming to reconstruct the damaged portion of such an historic home. The recent formation of the N.S.W. Heritage Council has given hope for future government action towards preserving Australia's heritage, and it is now up to the community to express its values and concern to the Heritage Council to enable the effective preservation of those sites significant to the district.

LIST OF REFERENCES

BOOKS

Australian Encyclopaedia. Editor in Chief; Alex H. Chisholm. Vol. 6.
Angus and Robertson Sydney. 1958.

Griffiths, G.N. *Some Houses and People of N.S.W.*
Ure Smith. Sydney. 1949.

Herman, Morton Earle. *The Architecture of Victorian Sydney.*
Angus and Robertson. Sydney. 1956.

Maxwell, C.F. (publishers) *Australian Men of Mark*
Sydney. 1889.

Palmer, Freda. *Lambridge to Castlereagh.*

Palmer, Freda. *Emu Hall.*

Palmer, Freda. *The Cottage, Mamre and Leeholme.*
Nepean District Historical Society.

Pike, Douglas (Ed.) *Australian Dictionary of Biography.* Vol. I. 1966.
Melbourne University Press.

ARTICLES, PAMPHLETS and MANUSCRIPTS.

Australian Leather Trades Review, March 1908.

Brabourne Collection, *Banks Papers,* Vol. 6.
Bligh 1805-1811   pp. 167-8, 174, 185-6.
Mitchell Library Collection.

Bertie, C.H. "Pioneer Families of Australia"   pp. 40, 70.
The Home, May, 1933.

Bigge, J.T. *Report Appendix*   pp. 3839-52, p. 6084, p. 6449.
Mitchell Library Collection.

Bigge, J.T. *Bonwick Transcripts,*   Appendix Vol. 123,133.
Mitchell Library Collection.

Bonwick Transcripts   Vol. 1 pp. 363-4
Vol. 4 pp. 1358-9
Mitchell Library Collection.

Bowers, Rev. William. "A Sketch of the History of the Parish of Mulgoa"   1911.
Watchman Newspaper Co. Ltd.
Mitchell Library Collection.

Brisbane, Sir Thomas. *Letter Book 1.*   pp. 89-93.
Mitchell Library.

Bunyan G. and Street, A. "The Nepean Valley and Penrith"
St. Marys—Penrith. — 1955.
Commemorating the Opening of
the Electric Railway to the District.

Byrnes, J.V. "Andrew Thompson   1773-1810".
Royal Australian Historical Society Journal and Proceedings.
Vol. 48.   Pt.2   pp 118-120.

Campbell, J.F. "Early Settlement on the Lower Nepean River, N.S.W."
Royal Australian Historical Society Journal and Proceedings
Vol. 18,   1932.   pp. 252-270.

Picture the soft glow from red glass oil lamps ... Perfume from Jasmine fills St. Thomas for a Spring Wedding.

Carroll, E. "Penrith Revisited" *Press Contributions*
        Vol. 1.   1904-1908.
        Mitchell Library Collection.

Cartledge, H. "History of Penrith: The First Fifty Years"
        Penrith Times.   3rd Nov., 1949
        Sept.-Dec. 1949.

Evans, Albert. *"Communicator No. 1"*   1968.

Evans, W. P. "Pioneers of the Textile Industry"
        Textile Journal of Australia.

Freame, William. "Lavender and Old Lace"
        Royal Australian Historical Society
        Journal and Proceedings.   1926.

Forde, J.N. "Early Penrith" *Newspaper Cuttings.*
        Vol. 92.   pp. 140.
        Mitchell Library Collection.

Gipps, Governor. *Transcripts of Missing Despatches to Lord Stanley*   1842-1843.
        Mitchell Library Collection

Gledhill, P.W. "A History of the Parish of Penrith"   1949.

James, R.E.H. "The Nortons of Sussex (England) and
        New South Wales"   Sydney.   1912.

Jamison, Thomas. Indenture from Thomas Jamison to Dr. John Jamison.
        Jamison Family Papers   pp. 5-8, pp. 9-24.

Jervis, James. "The Discovery and Settlement of Burragorang Valley"
        Royal Australian Historical Society Journal and Proceedings.
        Vol. 20.   pt. III   1934.

Jervis, James. "The Journals of William Edward Riley"
        Royal Australian Historical Society Journal and Proceedings
        Vol. 32   Pt. IV   1946.

Jervis, James. "Historical Notes and Queries"
        Royal Australian Historical Society Journal and Proceedings
        Vol. 35.   Pt. II.   p. 141.

King, H.W. "Penrith District Historical Survey"
        Nepean Times.   11th May, 1939.

King Papers. Vol. 6   pp. 60-3.
        Vol. 8.   pp. 76-8, 80-84.
        Mitchell Library Collection.

Mackaness, G. "Some Private Correspondence of the Rev. Samuel Marsden and
        Family. 1794-1824"   Sydney   D.S. Ford.   1942.

Macquarie, Lachlan. Despatch to Liverpool Oct. 27, 1810.
        Historical Records of N.S.W.   Vol. 7.   p. 347.
        Mitchell Library Collection.

Macquarie, Lachlan. *Government Despatch.*   No. 32.
        1st December, 1817.
        Mitchell Library Collection.

Macquarie, Lachlan. Macquarie's Memoranda.   p. 175.
        Nov. 30th, 1821.
        Mitchell Library Collection.

Marsden, K. "The Parson who Pioneered Australian Wool"
    Wool Record. 1964. p. 23

"Old Chum". "Old Sydney Column." *The Truth.*
    18/1/1920, 15/2/1920, 25/3/1920.

Penrith Methodist Circuit. "Centenary 1861-1961" Nov. 1961.
    Penrith City Library Collection.

Piper Papers. Vol. 2. pp. 165-166.
    Mitchell Library Collection.

Ramsden, Eric. "Marsden and the South Seas"
    Royal Australian Historical Society Journal and Proceedings
    Vol. 24. 1938.

Ramsden, Eric. *Marsden and the Missions; Prelude to Waitangi.*
    Angus and Robertson Ltd, Sydney. 1936.

Roxborough, Rachael. *Early Colonial Houses of New South Wales.*
    Ure Smith, Sydney. 1974.

Ryan, James T. *Reminiscences of Australia.*
    George Robertson, Sydney. 1894.

Steege, Joan. *Emu Plains.*
    Nepean District Historical Society. 1974.

Roberts, Rev. C.S. "Interesting Historical Relics around Penrith".
    Journal and Proceedings of the Parramatta Historical Society.
    Vol. III. 1926.

Street, A., Bunyan, G., and Whalan, R. "Pioneer Links of Township Penrith".
    Penrith Centenary 1871-1971.
    Penrith City Council 1971.

Sydney Gazette, March 13, 1833, April 24th, 1803.

Walker, F. "Penrith and District"
    Royal Australian Historical Society Journal and Proceedings
    Vol. 2. 1909.

Watson, J.H. "The Story of the Cox Family and the History of the Mulgoa
    and Penrith Districts"
    Nepean Times 11/7/1914.

Watson, J.H. "In Old Mulgoa" *Nepean Times* 24/10/1914.

Watson, J.H. "Mulgoa, Present and Past"
    Royal Australian Historical Society Journal and Proceedings
    Vol. IV, Pt. III. 1917.

Unpublished Articles.

Cox, M., and Woodriff, J. "Capt. Daniel Woodriff, C.B. R.N."
    Courtesy of Mrs. M. Cox.

Jamison, J.H. Talk given by the great grandson of Sir John Jamison.
    Penrith City Library Collection.

Lethbridge, John King. Notes on "Werrington House"
    Planning and Environment Commission,
    Sydney.

Pioneer Settlers of St. Marys — South Creek. Penrith City
    Library Collection.

"The Single Family of Summer Hill" courtesy of Mr. W.F. Single.

INDEX

AGNES BANKS	8, 77
Alcock, Alfred	70
Arms of Australia Inn	46, 48
Barnet, James	14
Bayley, Nicholas	58
Bayley, Nicholas Paget	58
Bayley Park	58
Beaston, Robert	45, 48
Bennett, James and George	76
Bennett Wagon	73
Bent, Ellis	55
Blackett, Cyril	18
Blackett, Edmund	55
Blaxland, Gregory	67
Bligh, William	7, 22, 58, 70, 77
Brisbane, Sir Thomas	2, 44
Bronte	73, 76
Brown, John	49
Cassola	2
CASTLEREAGH	1-12
Castlereagh Schools	5
Chapman, William Neate	12
Christ Church	6, 7
Cobb and Co.	48
Collett, Mary	5
Combewood	10
Cottage, The	30
Court House	14
Cox, Edward	18, 30
Cox, Edward King	30
Cox, George	18, 30, 34, 36
Cox, Henry	30, 36
Cox, Margaret	10
Cox, William	1, 7, 10, 30, 58
Craithes	2
Cram Place	16
Dibbs, Sir George	52
Dungarth	44
Donohue, Bold Jack	14
Edinglassie	53
Ellison, William	48
EMU PLAINS	44-54
Emu Hall	49
Emu Plains Prison Farm	1, 2, 45
Evans, James	48
Ewan, James	40
Fairlight	37
Fernhill	30
Field, E.	7
Fitzgerald, Richard	77
Fleurs	58
Flour Mills	12
Forbes, Sir Francis	53
Fraser, Alexander	5, 14
Fulton, Henry, Rev.	1, 7, 14, 18
Glenleigh	40, 41, 42, 43
Glenmore	36
Greendale Church	55
Harold, Father	1, 7
Hassell, Rev.	18, 36
Helleyer, W.	48
Hobartville	78, 79
Hogan, Michael	44, 49
Howell, W.	12
Huntington Hall	52
Jackson, William	53
Jamison, Sir John	14, 22, 36, 44
Jamison, Thomas	22
Jarrett, W.	37
Jones, Richard	63
King, Anna	70, 71
King, Mary	74
King, Phillip Gidley (Gov.)	1, 10, 22, 63, 70, 71
King Phillip Parker	70, 71
Lambridge	12
Lawson, Lt.	67
Leeholme	67
Lees, John	5
Lethbridge, Robert Copeland	7, 14, 36, 70, 74
LUDDENHAM TO MAMRE	55-69
Macarthur, John	63
Macquarie, Lachlan (Gov.)	22, 44, 70
Mamre	63
Marsden, Charles	18, 63
Marsden, Samuel, Rev.	2, 7, 18, 58, 63
Marsh, Rosetta	4
McCarthy, James	1
McHenry, John and Sarah	10, 14
Methodist Church: Castlereagh	5
Emu Plains	48, 53
Penrith	19
Mimosa	74
Mortimer, John	48
Mort, Thomas Sutcliffe	36
Mt. Pleasant	4
MULGOA VALLEY	30-43
Nepean Park	2
Nicholson, Sir Charles	58
Nixon St. Cottage	60
Norton, Nathaniel	37
O'Connell, Sir Maurice	70
Ormorde House	21
Osborne	77
Page, John	74
Parkes, Sir Henry	22, 52, 74
Parkes Platform	70
PENRITH	14-29
Putland, Mary	70
Putland, Lt.	70
Red Cow	22, 26
REGENTVILLE	22-26
Riley, James John	36
Riverside	52
Rodley	10
Ryan, James	5, 49
Sainsbury, James	74
Settlers Restaurant	65
Shadforth, Colonel	55
Single, John	2, 7
Single, Joseph	2, 7
St. Andrews	6, 7
St. James	58
St. Marks	55, 57
St. Marys	70-76
St. Pauls	45, 46
St. Stephens	18
St. Thomas	36
Tailby, George	52
Tailby's Hall	52
Terry, Samuel	4
Thompson, Andrew	77
Tindale, John	7, 19, 18
Union Inn	47, 48
Wardell, William	34, 38
Wentworth, George	7, 55
Wentworth, William Charles	7, 55, 58
Werrington House	72, 74
Werrington Park	68, 70, 71
Winbourne	34, 38
Woodriff, Capt. Daniel	10